JOCKS IN THE JUNGLE

JOCKS IN THE JUNGLE

The Second Battalion of the 42nd Royal Highland Regiment, The Black Watch and the First Battalion of the 26th Cameronians (Scottish Rifles) as Chindits

by

Gordon Thorburn

Pen & Sword
MILITARY

First published in Great Britain in 2012 by
Pen & Sword Military
an imprint of
Pen & Sword Books Ltd
47 Church Street
Barnsley
South Yorkshire
S70 2AS

ISBN 978 1 84884 792 7

A CIP catalogue record for this book is
available from the British Library

Typeset in Sabon by
Phoenix Typesetting, Auldgirth, Dumfriesshire

Printed and bound in England by
CPI Group (UK) Ltd, Croydon, CR0 4YY

Pen & Sword Books Ltd incorporates the Imprints of Pen & Sword Aviation,
Pen & Sword Family History, Pen & Sword Maritime, Pen & Sword Military,
Pen & Sword Discovery, Wharncliffe Local History, Wharncliffe True Crime,
Wharncliffe Transport, Pen & Sword Select, Pen & Sword Military Classics,
Leo Cooper, The Praetorian Press, Remember When, Seaforth Publishing and
Frontline Publishing

For a complete list of Pen & Sword titles please contact
PEN & SWORD BOOKS LIMITED
47 Church Street, Barnsley, South Yorkshire, S70 2AS, England
E-mail: enquiries@pen-and-sword.co.uk
Website: www.pen-and-sword.co.uk

Contents

Foreword

Families spend holidays where the rivers flow in Madhya Pradesh, north-central India. They have elephant rides and jungle drives, hoping to see a tiger.

In 1943, there was no thought of such good times for two battalions of Scottish soldiers. For them, that country meant a new and unimaginably arduous kind of training.

Some of the Black Watch boys had seen action in Somaliland, Crete and Tobruk. Some of the Cameronians had fought the Japs in the Burma retreat. Even for these, such training was trial by ordeal. Many more of the Jocks were new, just shipped out from Scotland, but all of them were ordinary men; men from the towns and villages who'd taken the King's shilling in their country's peril.

These were first-class British infantry, but not the super-selected Special Forces types that we know today. Nevertheless, it was a special-forces job they were supposed to do and that is what they were called, Special Force.

The challenge in Madhya Pradesh was to turn themselves into jungle fighters as good as the Japanese. They had a few short months to become Chindits.

They joined two brigades of 7,677 officers and men going into the jungle, of whom 531 were killed, captured or missing, and around 1,600 were wounded. By the end, some 3,800 were too sick to fight. Only 1,754 could be classified as 'effective' when they came out and, in truth, half of those were fit for no more than a hospital bed. It was a miracle anybody survived at all.

And that was just two of the five brigades that went in. Was this the greatest medical disaster of World War Two? Who caused it?

Author's Note

General Orde Wingate's 3rd Indian Infantry Division, called Special Force, as originally constituted and in training, was seven brigades plus various specialist units; the equivalent of thirty battalions and other forces, with most battalions divided into two columns. So, for example, 14 Brigade was four battalions from different regiments, in eight columns. Each column was about 400 hundred men.

One brigade in Chindit training was American and deployed elsewhere as the famous Merrill's Marauders, and one of the British brigades was also reassigned, so the 1944 Chindits went in as five brigades. The Cameronians' two columns in Number 111, and the Black Watch's two columns in Number 14 were, obviously, small parts of a greater whole, and concentrating on their stories is not meant to put them above or beyond anyone else. They were typically special, not especially special.

You may talk about your Lancers, and your Irish Fusiliers,
Your Aberdeen Militia and the Queen's Own Volunteers.
Of all the other regiments that's going far awa',
Just give to me the tartan of the gallant Forty Twa.

Strolling through the green fields on a summer's day,
Watching all the country girls working at the hay,
I really was delighted and he stole my heart awa'
When I saw him in the tartan of the gallant Forty Twa.
                    (Traditional, probably nineteenth century)

On the eighteenth day of April, in the year of forty four,
When the boys of the Cameronians went marching to the fore,
It was early in the morning as the Cams were standing to,
That they met and fought the enemy on the road to Pinlebu.

Now think of the fourteenth army, the boys who fought so well,
Of the hardships they had suffered, no-one but them can tell.
Far from their homes in Blighty and the folks they loved so true,
They fought and died forgotten, on the road to Pinlebu.
                    (Anonymous)

Dedication

Of course this book is dedicated to all the men who fought the Japanese in the Burmese jungle, but in particular to the ones I met and to whom I was privileged to listen: Pipe Corporal Bill Lark, Corporal Jim McNeilly and Colonel David Rose DSO. I only wish that their words to me could have been amplified and reinforced by words from my own father, Private/Rifleman 14254229 Andrew Douglas Thorburn, sometime Lance Corporal, who was there but never said a thing about it.

He joined the Black Watch at No 8 Infantry Training Centre, Queen's Barracks, Perth, on 16 September, 1942, where he was classified as a signaller and sent on to the Training Battalion, the 10th, on 30 December, stationed at Thurso, and then at Alnwick in Northumberland. He 'proceeded overseas' on 12 March, 1943, as part of a draft of 120 officers and men, and was in Bombay on 11 June.

The first Chindit expedition had begun in January 1943 and ended in April, and its initial success had resulted in a new Chindit Brigade being formed; the 111th Indian Infantry, made up of 1st Battalion Cameronians, 2nd Battalion King's Own, and 3rd Battalion of the 4th Gurkha Rifles.

The 120 Black Watch, sent to India for the purpose although not told so, were transferred to the Cameronians on 31 July to begin training in the jungle and eventually to fly in to Burma, 200 miles behind Japanese lines, with 111 Brigade, Special Force.

I am fortunate in having the personal account of an exact contemporary of my father, Frederick C. Patterson, Black Watch and Cameronians, on which to draw for this part of the history.

I say my father never spoke of it. Well, hardly ever. I can remember one occasion driving along in his car with the radio on, when the death of a man was announced. 'Good God above,' said my father. 'Last time I saw him was on Hill (whatever it was).'

He was six feet tall, my father, and 154lb (11st) when he joined the army. He came home from the jungle, after contracting amoebic dysentery, weighing a little over six stone. This was the only fact to become part of family history; that my father was six stone when he was 'invalided out', and is the reason why the medical disaster of the Chindits, usually neglected in telling the story, is such an important part of this book.

He recovered at a hospital in Southport, and went back into the police force he had volunteered to leave. For many, many, years afterwards, until eventually persuaded by my mother, he never would go abroad for holidays. Abroad, you see, was an awful place.

Gordon Thorburn, Autumn, 2011

Acknowledgements

Thanks to Mrs Terry Patterson for her help and permission to quote from her husband's memoirs, to Thomas B. Smyth, Black Watch Archivist, Barrie Duncan of the Cameronians Museum, Hamilton, and to Ken Stewart for information.

Chapter One

Religious Freedom

and Watching the Highlands

All famous regiments of the line can list great battles and brave deeds, but few can claim such unorthodox births as the Cameronians and the Black Watch. Both began with fierce loyalty to the Crown, but with a unique second reason for being.

The origins of the Cameronians are in the Scottish religious struggles of the (mainly) seventeenth century, and in the Presbyterian faith as practised in south west Scotland. The regiment arose out of the Covenanters, those who had signed or agreed with the three Covenants, which were also signed by the several kings, and which demanded freedom of worship and freedom from bishops. Charles II, although a signatory, declared the Covenants void and imposed bishops on the Scots, ejecting the local ministers if they would not submit. Covenanters followed their ministers who held services wherever they could, with armed guards to prevent interference from government forces.

Persecution was severe; its natural consequence, rebellion. Armed uprisings included one led by a most radical Covenanter called Richard Cameron. His death in battle at Airds Moss made him a folk hero and a particularly strict element of the Presbyterians began to call themselves Cameronians.

1

When the Catholic King James II of England and VII of Scotland was kicked out, to be replaced by the firmly Protestant William of Orange, one of the many results was the establishment of non-episcopal Presbyterianism as the official religion of Scotland. The formation of a Puritan regiment of foot swiftly followed in 1689, mustering beside the Douglas Water in Lanarkshire, and named the Cameronians for the Covenanter martyr, and professing certain religious leanings, with the young James Douglas, fourteenth Earl of Angus, as Colonel.

Every man had a bible, went to the kirk armed, and swore allegiance to the king, 'in defence of the nation' and 'in opposition to Popery'.

Earlier in that same year, John Graham, Viscount of Dundee (Bonny Dundee) had raised an army to fight the Stewart cause. He defeated loyalist forces at Killiekrankie, himself being slain just as victory was his. Without him as leader, the Jacobites moved on Dunkeld but failed to take it, even though it was a town without natural defensive assets, and the garrison – the Cameronian Regiment – was small. Well organised, the novitiates thus won their first action, withstanding the shock of the highland charge and gradually wearing down the Jacobites with disciplined firing.

The rebels retreated to the north and that was the end of the Jacobite threat for the moment. The Cameronians were soon posted abroad, to the Low Countries to oppose the French in the Nine Years War, and on to great honours in all the major wars thereafter.

Having had the same monarchs for a century, the Scottish parliament voted for complete union with England in 1707 – largely for economic reasons – during the reign of Queen Anne. When she died in 1714, her successor was the

2

Hanoverian George I, who couldn't speak English and hardly knew where Scotland was.

The Earl of Mar, without bothering to check first with the exiled James Stuart (the Old Pretender, son of James II), raised another Jacobite banner in 1715. As with Bonny Dundee's efforts, the rebellion might well have succeeded had it been better organised and directed after initial success, but it rather fizzled out at the battle of Sheriffmuir, fought between Mar's highlanders and the Duke of Argyle's loyalist army. Mar had much greater numbers but little experience as a military commander. Argyle had the professional soldiers, and the result was a fairly chaotic draw. For a description, we need go no further than the poetry of William McGonagall:

> *'Twas in the year 1715, and on the 10th of November,*
> *Which the people of Scotland have cause to remember;*
> *On that day the Earl of Mar left Perth bound for Sheriffmuir,*
> *At the same time leaving behind a garrison under Colonel*
>   *Balfour.*

> *Besides leaving a force of about three thousand men*
>   *quartered in different parts of Fife,*
> *To protect the people's property, and quell party strife,*
> *The army along with him amounted to three thousand foot*
>   *and twelve hundred cavalry,* (actually six thousand and
>   eight hundred respectively)
> *All in the best of order, a most pleasant sight to see.*

(To cut a long story short –
The battle swayed to and fro,
With the poet giving us lots of information, in line after line of piffle, that we don't need to know.)

3

Then the Highlanders chased them and poured in a volley,
Besides they hewed them down with their broadswords
*   mercilessly;*
But somehow both armies got mixed together, and a general
*   rout ensued,*
While the Highlanders eagerly the English (actually Scottish)
*   army hotly pursued.*

The success on either side is doubtful to this day,
And all that can be said is, both armies ran away;
And on whichsoever side success lay it was toward the
*   Government,*
And to allay all doubts about which party won, we must
*   feel content.*

By no means all the highland clans were Jacobite inclined.
For example, the Campbells, Grants, Frasers and Munros
were loyal to the crown and, when the dust had had time to
settle after Sheriffmuir, from among these families six companies of militia were formed, three of Campbells and one
each of the others. They were really a kind of armed police,
placed in small units at key points across the highlands, there
to keep the peace between the clans, maintain order and, as
far as was possible, enforce the laws of parliament which
prohibited men from carrying weapons.

Although run on clan lines, they did have a uniform of
sorts, plaids in sombre colours which from a distance looked
almost black, and which had nothing in common with the red
coats of the king's regulars. Their job was to watch for trouble
and so they acquired a nickname, the 'Black Watchers'.

Sheltering in France, the Stuarts remained a threat and a
focal point for unrest. Perhaps with this in mind, the six
companies, plus another four, were amalgamated and
formalised into a regiment of the army, with the restriction

that all recruits were to be Scots, 'and none other to be taken'.

George II's decree for this to happen was given in 1739. The regiment held its initial parade at the River Tay, near Aberfeldy, the following year, under the command of Colonel John Lindsay, twentieth Earl of Crawford. They now wore the red coat for the first time, with red waistcoat too, and a blue bonnet, above twelve yards of blue, green and red plaid wound about and held by an ox-leather belt four inches wide. They carried a musket, bayonet and broadsword, with a small shield and a choice of a pistol or dirk. Probably noting that you only had one shot with a pistol but could do more mischief quickly with the dagger, that's what most of them chose.

The Scots-only recruitment policy was interpreted by many of the men as Scotland-only in terms of duty, so when the regiment marched to London for a royal inspection, which didn't happen, and the rumour went about that they were for a West Indies posting, at least a hundred of them decided to go home. They were caught in Northamptonshire and, after courts martial, three of the ringleaders were shot.

Their role as a regular army regiment having been thus fully explained, several more things had to occur before they could become the Black Watch of legend. They had their first battle – against the French at Fontenoy in 1745 – and soon after that were allocated the 42nd rank of seniority in the British army and thus became, in Scots, the Gallant Forty-Twa.

The red hackle became part of the Black Watch uniform in 1795, and so the Forty Twa had all its identity and was ready to march into glorious history.

In 1779, another battalion was raised which shortly became the 73rd Regiment, which rejoined the 42nd in the reorganisation of 1881 as the Second Battalion of The Black Watch Royal Highland Regiment.

In 1794, a regiment of Perthshire Volunteers was raised to fight revolutionary France, which later became the Perthshire Light Infantry and 90th in seniority. In 1881 the Perthshires became the Second Battalion of the much older Cameronians, the 26th Regiment, and together were named The Cameronians (Scottish Rifles).

These numbers – 42, 73, 26 and 90 – were to prove significant in 1944.

Chapter Two

The Road to India

The 1st Battalion Cameronians were on police and training duties in Secunderabad, central Hyderabad province, when the urgent call came in early February 1942 to stop the Japanese taking the whole of Burma. They mobilized rapidly despite various equipment shortages, travelled to Madras and sailed into Rangoon harbour on 21 February. They found the city already deserted and moved to barracks at Mingladon, six miles outside.

Officers from GHQ briefed the Cams (whose CO was Lieutenant Colonel W. B. Thomas), and 2 IC Major R. M. H. Tynte. The situation was dire. All civil administration had broken down, including transport and telegraph, and there was significant anti-British sentiment among the locals in the countryside around. Japs and their Burman allies were massing by a bridge on the Sittang River, some ninety miles north-east of Rangoon, so the Battalion moved to Pegu (modern Bago), a large town on its own river, forty miles short of that point, to form up ready to march on the Sittang bridge.

No sooner had they arrived than orders came to go back to Rangoon to quell rioters and looters. Then more orders told them to stay put and take up defensive positions around Pegu, including the villages of Payagyi and Waw, both roughly fifteen miles further on towards the enemy. The bridge by now had been blown, with most of the British and Indian forces on the wrong side, the east side, of the Sittang.

Over the next few days the Cams watched a continuous stream of refugee soldiers who had had to swim the Sittang and walk twenty-five miles through inhospitable country to get to Waw and safety. Meanwhile, Cams patrols encountered Burman snipers and bandits, as well as regular Japanese troops, who seemed to be able to move through the jungle and appear and disappear without difficulty.

It was becoming obvious that the Japs greatly outnumbered the Imperial forces and despite courageous counter-attacks and many skirmishes, retreat to Pegu from the outlying positions seemed inevitable. Air attacks too were increasing, with a consequent decrease in air support for the defenders. On one counter-attack, for example, support from twenty Blenheim fighter-bombers was promised but only two turned up.

By 6 March the Japs were in Pegu, holding the railway station and setting up road blocks. Confusion reigned, with much close-quarters fighting and constant reports of detachments of Gurkhas, West Yorks, 7th Hussars, Essex Yeomanry and others, having successes and failures as they tried to stop the unstoppable. One small unit of the Cameronians, while extricating a broken-down Bofors gun, was surprise-attacked by Japs and most of its members killed; the dead Scots having their heads removed and stuck on poles.

A determined assault by the Cams and others blasted the Japs out of Pegu station but they were soon back, with thousands of reinforcements coming up.

A reporter for the *Daily Mirror*, T. E. A. Healy, was in Rangoon. Here is an extract from his dispatch:

'I wanted to go up to front line headquarters . . . during the battle of Pegu, which was also the battle of Rangoon.

I got there in a scooter-type Ford two-seater which is known as a Jeep.

'HQ were surprised that I had got along the road without being shot at, because Japanese snipers had been firing on almost every vehicle on the road for twenty-four hours . . . they agreed to let me go still nearer the front towards the headquarters of a famous Scottish regiment.'

He watched the retaking of the railway station, but that was the last little victory for a while:

'With amazing speed, the fighting spread from this isolated patch of jungle to almost a half-circle (from which) came bursts of Japanese mortar and tommy-gun fire. Our troops were quickly dispatched on patrols, advancing with admirable courage straight into the undergrowth and the jungle. The air was filled with crackling duels and the situation seemed gradually worsening for us. Bullets sang and whined above.

'We had to face the grim fact – we were cut off. And as the circle of battle gradually shrunk, I thought that a slit throat was my fate not many hours away.

'A dispatch rider raced past the snipers to say that a brigade was on its way to relieve us. All afternoon we waited for that relief column. It never arrived. The Japanese held the road too strongly and they built formidable road blocks through which the relief could not pass.

'The Hindoo temple, which had been our HQ, was now the casualty station. HQ was out in the paddy field.'

Healy helped with the wounded, taking off tunics and boots ready for the surgeon. The Jap air force arrived and dive-bombed. Healy briefly joined up with the Hussars and their tanks forcing their way through a roadblock to escape northwards:

'But whatever happened, Pegu was finally lost, and the Burma Road – along which so much aid had travelled to China – was gone. Lost, too, was Rangoon – for even as Pegu fell, our forces quitted Rangoon.'

The British were heavily dependent on motor transport and therefore, on the few roads, while the Japanese were trained and practised in moving in the jungle, going round rather than through the defenders' positions, and leap-frogging the retreating forces ready to block their way. Withdrawal from Pegu was ordered, counter-ordered and ordered again, with the Cams and the West Yorks forming the rearguard as the outmatched Burma Army set off north for Prome.

Assaults on Jap roadblocks met with some success and at great cost, only for more blocks to be set up. A favourite joke of the Japs if they took a prisoner, was to tie him to the barrier, knowing that his own side would kill him in trying to burst through.

The road was the only way, but the Japanese held the country on both sides of it and attacked anything that moved along it. One platoon of the Cameronians headed north along the railway line instead, and met a very large force of the enemy. After a fierce battle with losses on both sides, the Cams turned south and walked all the way to Rangoon which, of course, was Jap-held by this time. The officer, Captain P. V. Gray, split his men into small parties and turned back north. Most of them managed to evade the Japs, often walking through the middle of enemy formations. Some rejoined the Battalion, some found their way back to India.

A young Second Lieutenant of the Cameronians, not named, told his part in that story:

'Orders came to withdraw (from Pegu) after we were completely surrounded, and as leading platoon of the leading

10

company, we set out. We were advancing down a railway line . . . when out of the mist appeared a large force of unknown soldiers . . . we challenged them, still thinking they might be some of our own native troops. Immediately, they opened up with everything they had, at point-blank range. They were screaming like demons.

'You could see the tracer bullets hitting people all around you, and feel the whistle of them past your own body. Then they charged with bayonets and double-handed swords. Our fellows fought magnificently, and we gave them as good as we got.

'Eventually we withdrew, as did the enemy, but the damage was done and contact was lost with our own troops.'

They turned back towards Rangoon, hoping to meet up with friendly forces but instead, after two days and nights of marching, walked into the city to find the Japs in possession. For the next four days they wandered around without map or compass, trying to find a road out:

'On the seventh day (we walked) through a Japanese HQ, but we got away without being noticed. There were only four of us by this time.'

The four were two RAOC, the Lieutenant and a Cameronian sergeant. They joined up with another small party, dodged the Japs and the bandits for a fortnight, and hitched a ride aboard a refugee ship to India.

For the rest, the way back to India looked a hard road indeed. Motor vehicles and tanks were becoming a liability, so often were they knocked out by the enemy and turned into yet more blocks. Communications, which relied on transport, were worsening, and by 8 March the Battalion was the advance guard, and the Second-in-Command, Richard Tynte – lately Lieutenant Colonel – was dead.

They had fought around Pegu for three weeks. The next three were spent gradually moving north, halting and digging

11

in for a day here, two days there, with little enemy contact, until they reached the Prome area, where there were several expensive battles, during which the British were subjected to much dive-bombing from Jap aircraft; the enemy now having total air superiority.

William Mundy of the *News Chronicle* was there:

'At dawn, British troops on the Irrawaddy front launched an offensive which by nightfall had captured Paungde, smashed two Japanese battalions, and was sweeping on towards Okpo . . . for the first time in Burma, the British made the decision to turn defence into offence, partly with the aid of the Chinese, who were counter-attacking strongly in the Toungoo valley.

'All around me officers and men were saying, "At last we are going the right way." And when bombs rocked the earth and bullets spluttered viciously down, they still said, "Well, anyway, we are going the right way."

'Once when I sought shelter, a Cameronian with a Bren gun, pacing impatiently up and down, his eyes glued on the Japanese fighters flashing in the sun further down the road, lamented, "They never come near me. I've never had a chance to use this bloody gun yet."'

Reporter T. E. A. Healy was there too, to see the thrust south from Prome succeed:

'But behind them, events were developing fast. Defeated for the moment, the Japs threw large reinforcements of their troops and the Burmans into battle . . . bombers and fighter aircraft were thrown in, and the weight of their bombs and bullets tilted the scale against us.

'Thirty miles of that road was marked and numbered by the bodies of gallant soldiers who had given all . . .

12

The most incredible character, perhaps, was the Cameronian driving a Bren gun carrier, who was shot through the cheek. He spat the bullet on the floor of the carrier (saying) "That bloody bullet bounced off my teeth."'

Individual heroism cannot, alas, bring down aircraft nor repel hugely superior artillery bombardment, and Prome had to be abandoned in the knowledge that the Japanese, using their tactic of going round rather than through, were attempting to block the road to the north.

On 31 March the Battalion, reduced to around 200 officers and men, harboured six miles north of Prome, but had to move on again two days later, heading for an Irrawaddy crossing point twenty-three miles north, hoping to get there before the Japs. They were bombed on the way and arrived exhausted, but were able to rest, wash, and recover for a while, before moving on to Magwe. Ten days later, on 16 April, the Japs were closing in and another withdrawal was ordered, with more roadblocks expected on route and strong enemy positions to be cleared.

After a major battle around Twingon and Yenaungyaung, the next objective was Myingyan, mostly by forced march, and the Chindwin River. More battles and rearguard actions saw them in Yeu, sixty or so miles north-west of Mandalay, where they received the order to withdraw to India.

By early May, the Chinese forces sent down by Chiang Kai-Shek had been driven back on the eastern flank as far as Myitkyina, and Jap advances to the west meant certain defeat for the British and Indians, who had no choice but to somehow struggle back to Assam before the enemy and the monsoon made such a thing impossible.

The Cameronians were much reduced, like the other regiments, a major cause being an enemy that hadn't really come in to the calculations – malaria. There had also been cases of dysentery, and lack of proper supplies for weeks had diminished many individuals as fighting men. Even so, they had also learned that the Japanese were not invincible. The campaign was a defeat – a retreat that became known as the longest in British military history, 900 miles from Rangoon to the Indian border – but reverses had been inflicted here and there. Another chance to hurt the Japs would come along soon. Now they had the roads and the railway, and needed them for supplies and communications. The leap-frogging road-block tactic would one day be adapted by Wingate's Chindits and turned against the enemy who invented it.

The last gasp of this campaign was the race to Shwegyin – the ferrying place across the Chindwin – along a road that would become useless for motor transport when the monsoon rains arrived. Food was another problem; there would be supplies along the way but not enough if the men were held up. A further possibility was a move up-river by the Japs, to set up a block that would cut off the retreat entirely.

The crossing for the Cams was a slow business on 8 May by small paddle steamer, and almost all of the vehicles had to be left behind. Still the Battalion was not done. It had escorting and guarding duties as the rest of the force made its weary way towards India. The rains came and hardly stopped. Malaria struck hard. Spirit alone could not compensate for sickness, inadequate rations and sheer exhaustion. At last, on 18 June, the remainder of the 1st Cams was ordered to move out of Burma. What had been a full-strength Battalion was scarcely a company in numbers, but they had played a major role in buying precious time, and helped prevent a total disaster.

The Black Watch Second Battalion embarked at Southampton in August 1937, heading for Palestine, having had six months' warning of the posting. The job would be internal security; not thought to be especially onerous. Among the Jocks was James McNeilly, piper William Lark, and a 25-year-old officer called David Rose. More of these men later. Already there in Jerusalem was Captain Orde Charles Wingate. More of him later, too.

Although operational paths were not fated to cross just yet, it was a small force and people were aware of each other – Jim McNeilly: 'I saw Wingate in Palestine. I met him, in 1938. He was a soldiering man. An all right man. He would never ask you to do something he couldn't do himself.'

The Jocks did not go to Jerusalem as notified, but to a camp about nine miles out of Jaffa. Neither did their pleasant sunshine holiday materialise because gangs of Arab rebels, increasingly active as more and more Jewish immigrants poured in from Europe, began blowing things up and assassinating officials. Pursuing these guerrillas proved to be very good training, physically, militarily, and in personal growth, maturity and decision-making among the previously untried young officers and NCOs.

It so happened that when hostilities in Europe began, Palestine was fairly quiet and war seemed remote. By early 1940, Italy looked sure to enter, with promise of action for the Black Watch, and the excitement started with an order received on 2 May. There was no peacetime six months' notice; they were to move to the Suez Canal on 3 May.

They kept the canal safe for a couple of months until another order came on 30 June which put them on a troopship, HMS *Liverpool*, next morning. Off they went to Aden, where they waited for the expected Italian invasion of Somaliland which, at that time, was divided into three colonies, French, Italian and British. The French authorities decided they would be Vichy rather than Free French, which left the British on their own to wonder what to do about their colony and, in particular, its capital Berbera.

The Italian invaders massively outnumbered the British in men, weapons and air support, but they had to come through mountain passes which might be defended. The Second Battalion, after some to-ing and fro-ing, was settled in a forward position near one of the passes, on a hill range called Barkasan. As more and more information came to HQ about the size and scope of the Italian army, the task switched from trying to keep the Italians out, to holding them long enough for a retreat and abandonment of the colony.

The Jocks and the Italians met for the first time on 13 August. A-Company was to escort a supply train further forward to positions at Tug Argan – at night and along the only road. The moonlit convoy of trucks was under the command of a fearsome disciplinarian known universally as 'Major KG', as his real name was Major Lindsay-Orrock-Graham-Scott. Up front were two Bren carriers; in the middle was Major KG; at the back was the Second-in-Command, Captain David Rose.

David Rose: 'We had only gone a few miles when we suddenly came under heavy fire. Ambush. The convoy bunched up. A lot of the African drivers ran away and I had to find replacements from among the Jocks. I worked my way up the convoy seeing to this, which I could do because most of the Italian firing was high, going over us, till I came to Major KG having his head bandaged. He'd fallen out of his truck, banged his head and got himself concussed, which meant I was now OC. I thought I should be in the leading truck so I made for that, to find the driver shot through the head and the road blocked by the wreck of a Bren carrier.'

Both obstacles were pulled out of the way and Rose got in the truck. He put his foot down and kept it down, learning as he went how to handle a type of vehicle he'd never driven before:

'All of a sudden there were lots of chaps waving their arms

16

about. I stopped to hear what they had to say. The gist of it was that I was in the minefield. So I reversed, keeping the wheel dead straight.'

The chaps in question were of the North Rhodesian Regiment, which had seen some hard fighting. A few days before it had had to withstand a cavalry charge and the dead horses and men were still lying around.

David Rose: 'There was a terrible smell but they all seemed quite used to it. Anyway, after a bit of a contretemps with a rather disagreeable colonel who had turned up from somewhere, during which I offered him command of the convoy – he refused – we set off back again. My orders were highly specific, along the lines of, "Take a spare driver for every lorry and keep going," and so we did. A cloud came over the moon, and we drove through the same ambush place with only one machine gun having a go at us.'

The convoy reached Barkasan scatheless, and Captain Rose reported to Brigade HQ.

'Who are you?' asked the Brigadier.

'A-Company, sir,' said Rose. The Brigadier was surprised, as the runaway drivers had already given him their own report.

'Your African drivers are here,' he said. 'They told me. Major killed. Captain wounded. All finish, no good.'

The Jocks were now given a very definite task: to hold the Barkasan ridge until the night of 17 August, which meant keeping the pass between the hills. Defensively, it wasn't much of a pass, being about two miles wide with low rising ground on either side, and the Battalion was not well equipped for the job. They had no machine guns, no heavy weaponry to speak of, and no air support.

David Rose: 'I had four Bren carriers and a section of three-inch mortars, which is to say two mortars and a few rounds. From our trenches on the western side, my company covered

17

the roadblock, which consisted of one platoon with the only Bofors gun and a dozen shells.'

Meanwhile, the VIPs in Berbera had been evacuated and the town garrison was also embarking. As day broke on 17 August at Barkasan, peace was disturbed only by a stray couple of platoons of Punjabi soldiers who were looking for a home.

David Rose: 'Then some Italian motor cyclists appeared, followed by trucks of troops. If only we'd had machine guns, we could have done for the lot of them. As it was, we opened up with rifle fire and caused chaos, with lorries reversing and motorcycles charging about, but more trucks were coming up behind.'

The Italians tried to advance against D-Company on the other side of the road, but were sent back and the day settled into a long process of Italian build-up and infiltration, with the occasional action from the Jocks if the enemy came too close.

David Rose: 'I shouted to the men to fix bayonets and come with me. Then we were all shouting, and charging at the enemy. It was very exciting. My hands were shaking which made reloading my pistol difficult, not that it mattered much because nothing seemed to happen to anyone I shot at. I vowed to bring a rifle next time. We went on and on, killing some but not many. I wondered if my whole company were just as bad shots as I obviously was.

'Somebody on the other side was better because I went arse-over-tip with a bullet through my shoulder. The "Blackshirts" (the better Italian troops) we had overrun started to pop up and fire at us, so we retreated to our trenches and I had to have my wound seen to.'

The value of the bayonet charge was not so much in the casualties inflicted, as in the psychological effect that fifty screaming mad Jocks had had on troops who had not experienced such a thing before. The enemy was now reluctant to engage until success was guaranteed, and so more and more reinforcements arrived, including tanks, machine guns and truckload after truckload of men.

Had the Italians deployed their greatly superior forces properly, there can be no doubt that the Second Battalion, almost out of ammunition and almost surrounded, would have been wiped out and/or forced to surrender. In fact, the news back at HQ, later on, was that they had been.

The enemy's modus operandi seemed to be to send in conscripted local troops pushed from behind by regular Italian soldiers, while tanks ran up and down the line to no positive purpose. The Black Watch could hold firm against such tactics, but not for ever. As the enemy forces increased, so did their confidence. Tanks were brought to bear and the Blackshirts were featuring more. In all, the Italians built up to five brigades.

The order came at 5.30pm for the Second Battalion to withdraw two miles down the road. The Italians did not follow and, with new orders, the Jocks kept on going all the way to Berbera. Piper Bill Lark was there, with C-Company:

'I had never before seen a soldier on a camel that was in full flight. It was a great sight to see at ground level, but must have been very hard on the backside of the poor jockey. If they had gone any faster they would have ended up in the Yemen.'

Thirty-six hours later, Lark, McNeilly, Rose and the rest, were all in Aden, and a week after that they were in Suez, except for the wounded, including Rose who was on a hospital ship. They took him to Delhi, where he heard the news from *The London Gazette* of 29 November 1940, that the King had been pleased to approve the award of the Distinguished Service Order to Captain David McNeil Campbell Rose of the Black Watch (Royal Highland Regiment).

'In my opinion I was over-decorated for a very junior officer, and I was rather shy about it.' The full citation perhaps emphasises David Rose's modesty:

'Captain David McNeil Campbell Rose in Somaliland for conspicuous gallantry during the action at Barkasan on August 17 1940. Captain Rose was commanding 'A' company. His company was hard-pressed by greatly superior enemy forces and it appeared that his company's locality would be overrun and the centre of the Battalion pierced, giving the enemy access to the main Berbera road. With great presence of mind and showing the highest courage this officer personally led a bayonet charge with his HQ and 1 Platoons and effectively routed the enemy. This action succeeded in checking the enemy and had a direct bearing on the result of the battle, enabling the original front to be maintained. His coolness, resource and high courage set an outstanding example to his men. During the bayonet charge Captain Rose was wounded in the shoulder. He remained in command until the situation was restored and was then evacuated to RAP (Regimental Aid Post). Recommended by Major A. Gilroy commanding 2nd Battalion Black Watch, signed A. R. Godwin-Austen and A. P. Wavell.'

After a few weeks of security duties in Cairo, the Battalion, minus Captain Rose, was sent to Crete on 19 November. At first, this seemed like an idyllic posting; no fighting in paradise, with all the locals anxious to be as hospitable as possible. There was work to do, of course, preparing the defences, but stressful it was not.

Bill Lark: 'There was a piper assigned to each Company, who had the rank of Piper. There were others who piped in the band but not with that rank. In action, they put their pipes away. Only the Company Piper kept his pipes. I was C-Company Piper. Our Company Commander was George Garden Green, just a Captain then. Later on I was made up to Pipe Lance Corporal and Pipe Corporal. HQ Company had a Pipe Major and a Pipe Sergeant. Willie Michie was on D-Company, Chan McCulloch on C, and I took over from Chan; Willie Morrison A-Company, Jake Ogilvie B-Company. We played the calls, jankers, lights out, reveille and all the rest of it. We played "A man's a man for a' that, though a man gets sixty days he's still a man for a' that". Sometimes on Crete there was an early air raid, so we had to wait for that to finish before we could play reveille.

'We had a man called "Sixty Scott" – that's how you knew him from the other Scotts – so we all called him "Sixty"; never knew him by any other name. We had a McGoff and a McGough, so on pay parade one was "McGoff eff eff", and the other was "McGough McGooch". They all called me "Brother Lark", because I was religious, didn't smoke or drink or go with women. I used to go to the local Christian mission in the town. They'd take me in and feed me. I had a great time there, but the other lads, they were going into town to get boozed up and meet the girls.'

In the spring, as matters became more and more desperate on mainland Greece, the defence of a fabulous island became a very serious business. Reinforcements arrived but they didn't seem to equate to the amount of effort the Germans were putting in. Although the original garrison at brigade strength, about 3,500 troops, was greatly amplified by Empire and Greek forces retreating from the mainland, so that eventually there were ten times the numbers, these could not be classified as combat ready. There was little or no equipment for a major defensive action. Even more important, there was no air force to speak of. German air superiority was almost total.

The defenders had another, unquantifiable disadvantage, in that they were being commanded from far away. The new man on the ground was General Bernard Freyberg VC, who had come to Crete from Greece with his New Zealand Division, but the C-in-C, General Archibald Percival Wavell, and his staff, were in Cairo, where they looked all around them and wondered how on earth they were going to defend the entire Middle East, north Africa and the Mediterranean with so little in the way of resources.

On 2 May Freyberg signalled Wavell that his forces 'can and will fight, but without full support from navy and air force cannot hope to repel invasion'. Wavell's reply cannot have heartened anyone:

'The Commander-in-Chief, Mediterranean, is prepared to support you if Crete is attacked. I have most definite instructions from the War Cabinet to hold Crete and, even if the question were reconsidered, I am doubtful if the troops could be removed before the enemy attack. The difficulties and dangers of your situation are fully realised, but I am confident that you and the magnificent troops at your disposal will be equal to the task. We have very anxious times ahead in the Middle East for the next few weeks.'

Commanders-in-Chief rarely say 'Stop bothering me and get on with it' directly, but the message was received and understood. Near-daily German air raids resembled the artillery barrage before the big advance, concentrating on their main objectives, the naval base at Suda Bay and the aerodromes. The Jocks were detailed to look after Heraklion aerodrome, recently completed, but with only a very few friendly aircraft stationed on it. It would be a prize for the enemy but not much of an asset to the defenders.

The air raids increased with bombs and strafing. Surely,

everyone thought, something must happen soon, but the barrage went on. At last, on 16 May, came the biggest air raid yet, followed by several days of relative quiet. In the afternoon of 20 May, a message came through that parachutists were dropping at the other completed aerodrome, Maleme, where the Battalion had previously been stationed.

It was a late message. Around 2,000 paratroops had descended on Maleme, with additional infantry landing on the beaches and elsewhere by glider. By the middle of the day, they had the airfield and could welcome German transport planes onto it.

Meanwhile, another massive air raid had to be suffered at Heraklion, with very little possibility of response. When that cleared, the biggest fleet of enemy aircraft anyone had seen rolled in like a black tidal wave. If that was not astonishing enough, eyes opened even wider in disbelief as the aerial cargo was discharged. The Battalion's War Diary describes what happened next, in poetical vein:

'The relief of the defenders was unbounded and a hail of fire greeted the enemy slowly descending like gigantic snowflakes on a breathless day. The fight was now on greater terms of equality. Within 24 hours, the Germans who had fallen inside the perimeter were dead or prisoner, and those outside had been badly mauled. It was no uncommon sight to see two men marching a dozen Germans with their hands up, through our lines.'

The drop carried on for two hours, and many Germans landed beyond the immediate reach of the Battalion, making themselves secure for the moment. Next day was a repeat performance, and the next and the next, except that the enemy now knew where not to drop. From information gathered later, it seemed that they had not expected the aerodrome to be occupied.

There were eight days of it. Heraklion aerodrome and its surrounding positions held firm, but everywhere else the battle had been lost. The mood among the officers and men of the Black Watch changed, from exhilaration at inflicting huge damage on the enemy, to that kind of fatalism which is usually described as 'grim determination'. They were going to have to fight to the last, and there was no expectation of getting away.

In that bleak outlook they were wrong. The Royal Navy was coming to get them at night on 28 November. The Germans were not to get a sniff of the evacuation or it would fail, and somehow, most of the Battalion did reach Heraklion harbour along with their reinforcement comrades of the Argylls and the Yorks and Lancs. Some outposts could not be contacted so they had to be left to fend for themselves.

The navy destroyers and cruisers had to run for it, in easy reach of the Luftwaffe stationed on Rhodes and mainland Greece. The attacks were incessant and successful, in particular two hits scored by Stuka dive bombers on cruisers HMS *Orion* and HMS *Dido*, which caused many casualties.

The Battalion's losses on Crete were fifteen men and two officers, with no ground given. On the journey back to safety in Alexandria, 200 were killed and more wounded. Even so, it can be said with certainty that the German score was far greater – many times greater. So big were the losses that Hitler never again tried such an airborne invasion.

We can also say that had the evacuation not been achieved, as in Somaliland there would have been nothing left of the Battalion for any further part in the war.

Bill Lark: 'The *Dido* steamed in to Alexandria at night, and one of my fellow pipers – Collins he was called – somehow got himself up on the bridge and began playing. He had his kilt on too; what was left of it. Some of the other ships put searchlights on him, and kept them on as the *Dido* came in. Not a dry eye in the house.'

After some leave and time to regroup and re-equip, the Battalion was ordered to Syria. The expectation was a fierce battle against the Vichy French who were installed very securely in a mountain fastness, but it never happened. After losses elsewhere, the Vichy French offered armistice terms and an oasis of peace appeared in the Middle East which was otherwise in turmoil. From mid-July to mid-September 1941, the Jocks managed to acclimatise to Syrian summer as they had managed in Crete, but the bill for their holidays was about to come in.

Axis forces were in the ascendancy in north Africa and had besieged Tobruk, on the Libyan coast near the Egyptian border. The Battalion was to relieve the Australian garrison in this most unpromising position; a natural harbour that had no natural defensive features inland. Fortifications were all man-made, and the town was a dump.

After a dangerous but unmolested run-in – courtesy of fast navy warships – the rapid handover had an unusual aspect.

Bill Lark: 'It had been decided to keep the pipers quiet, so that the enemy wouldn't hear us and know we'd arrived. So instead of the usual, Jake Ogilvie played on just his chanter, pianissimo, you might say. Our time would come, though.'

Tobruk had become a symbol of British and Empire bravery and cussedness, but it was a dismal posting. Everything was in short supply. Hardly a day passed without a dust storm and an air-raid. Living conditions were foul, so the latest news – that the Battalion was to be a spearhead of a breakout – was regarded as good, on the whole.

The Eighth Army was coming and the Tobruk garrison was to attack various entirely flat bits of desert, with tank support, while the enemy was in a state of utter confusion. Positions were silently taken up on the night of 20 November, ready for the strike at 06.30.

The time came, but there were no tanks. The Jocks went in, the tanks turned up but got lost, and men were mown down by machine guns as if it were the Somme all over again. Bayonet charges overran enemy positions but at huge expense. The attack slowed, as it was bound to, and might even have come to a stop but for the pipes.

Bill Lark: 'The Pipe Major struck up with "Hielan' Laddie", and we joined in with that, and I remember "The Black Bear", which was always played when a gee-up was needed. It seemed to work, but I also remember the dreadful effects of the German machine guns in their fixed line as we advanced. They caused us a lot of casualties. I was told by one officer to put away my pipes and pick up a rifle. His comment was "This isn't 1914", which made me very cross at the time. But there was a sort of sense in it, because we pipers were targets to be hit.'

A great many men were hit; so many that the order to stop where they were until tanks arrived was given. According to the War Diary, the Battalion was thirty officers and 580 men when the break-out began. As a controlled fighting force it was now down to five officers and 160 men who, with the armour reinforcements, took their final objective after an advance of three miles.

Black Watch casualties altogether in these few hours of action were eight officers and 108 men killed, and seventeen officers and 200 men wounded. It is not possible to say what the score was on the other side, but surely the enemy lost as many if not more, and the Jocks we know took almost 500 prisoners.

The Black Watch stayed in the old Italian and German positions for eighteen days, during which time Tobruk was again briefly isolated, but by 9 December it was clear that the Allies had won a victory and the Axis forces were in retreat. The Battalion moved back into Tobruk and, as New Year dawned, they were taken by motor transport to Egypt.

Ten days was the standard amount of leave, followed by another trip to Syria, where a German attack was always expected but never came. It was a short stay; too short, it would seem, for certain matters to be properly resolved in the officers' mess:

'TO THE HEAD QUARTER OF BRITISH GOVERNMENT, DAMASCUS.

Sir, I undersigned Ibrahim Akkad living at Damascus, Souk El Atik No 6, contractor of vegetables and fruits, has the honour to state that I have purveyed the Officers of the second Black Watch with different food stuffs, and this Unity having moved recently to an unknown place, without discharging its debts, specified as below. I beg your Excellence to make your order that my debts will be payed.'

The poor man had indeed supplied foodstuffs on six consecutive days in February, worth over 90 piastres. The bill was checked by a representative of His Excellence and marked 'Forward to 70 Division', with consequences we cannot know but can probably guess. Worse was to follow, placed at the door of one particular and famous officer of this unity, Bernard Fergusson:

'Damascus, July 7th 1942.

Dear Sir,

On February 1942 Major B E Fergusson of 2nd Bn Black Watch ordered me to make a silk flag for his Bn but on the 22nd of February I received a letter from him saying that he was leaving Syria but I had to forward to

27

him the said flag as soon as it was done and that he was ready to pay the cost of the flag and all expenses.'

The writer, whose name has been lost, finished the flag, took it into the office of military police and paid 75 piastres for postage to the Major.

'On April I wrote a letter to the Area Commander explaining the case, and there they told me that my letter would be forwarded to Major Fergusson as soon as possible. Five months have already passed and I am still waiting for an answer. The cost of the flag and the embroideries done amount to Syrian 125 plus the expense of the postage. Being a poor worker this sum is for me a small capital. I trusted blindly the Major . . . but we are in war time and nobody knows what may happen.'

You never said a truer word, Mr Flagman. Ibrahim Akkad's last fruit and veg delivery was on 21 February, 1942. Rommel was pushing forward against the Allies and regaining lost ground in north Africa, and when the Battalion got its movement orders everyone was quite sure that's where they were going; back to Tobruk or some equally welcoming hellhole. They boarded the train on 22 February at Damascus but it didn't take them to Cairo. Four days later they were sailing down the Gulf of Suez and into the Red Sea, on board the *Mauretania*.

Word soon went around about their destination: Rangoon, Burma. This, everyone knew, was at one end of the road to Mandalay, where the flying fishes play, and the dawn comes up like thunder out of China 'cross the bay, but that was about it. By the time they were out in the open Indian Ocean, Rangoon had fallen to the Japanese and their destination became Bombay, whence they moved inland to Ahmadnagar, then across the subcontinent to Bihar province and the jungle of Ranchi.

This was early April 1942. Duties were fairly non-specific for the Battalion which was part of the mobile reserve charged with the defence of India against the seemingly unstoppable Japanese, but that changed in the August. India's Congress Party was demanding independence from Britain. The British position was that such matters would be settled in whatever way the Indian people wanted when the war was over. On 8 August, Congress demanded that the British 'quit India' immediately. If the demand was refused, there would be 'mass struggle on non-violent lines on the widest possible scale'. Gandhi, Nehru, and the other leaders, were all arrested overnight and imprisoned, many in the fort at Ahmadnagar.

The struggle did not erupt on a wide scale. Most people, including the Indian armed forces, carried on as before, sure that the demand to quit was no more than another card played in the long game, and equally certain that life under the British was rather better than life would be under the Japs.

So, there was very little non-violence but there was quite a lot of violence, and the Battalion was detailed to keep the peace, first where they were in Bihar province, and then in Bengal. They settled at Contai, by the Ganges delta, where internal security suddenly became an entirely different matter on 16 October. Torrential rain during the night was followed by a cyclonic wind and a tidal wave which overwhelmed all defences and destroyed everything before it, except the strongest buildings on the highest ground.

Nobody had heard the word 'tsunami' in those days, but that's what it was. The War Diary described the scene on the morning of 18 October:

'Palms, strongest of trees, had been uprooted or bent at right angles by the force of the wind, entire villages had been swept away, and vast stretches of country were submerged. Dead humans and animals were everywhere.'

The death toll was in the many thousands and the Battalion's new role was disaster relief, reconstruction and mass burials. The Jocks' own losses, fourteen men drowned in the storm, were forgotten for the moment as labours of Hercules were performed every day for ten days, until the posting came further inland to Kharagpur. Three more weeks of internal security were followed by transfer back to Ranchi and to training.

Over the winter and spring, the Japanese threat to India increased. In May 1943, the Battalion moved to the curiously-named seaport of Cox's Bazaar in the southernmost little finger of Bengal (now Bangladesh), close to the border with Burma and the province of Arakan.

Patrols were mounted into Jap-occupied territory and first contact with the enemy was made south of Buthidaung, fifteen miles or so beyond the border. The Jocks came across a temporarily unoccupied position, waited until the occupiers came back from the river where they were bathing, and then gave them a warm welcome. It was the first Japanese blood to the Battalion, at no cost.

Extract from the American *Intelligence Bulletin* (January 1944):

'A high-ranking British officer stated that the major slogan for jungle warfare against the Japanese is "Patrol! Patrol! Patrol!" A patrol, he said, must avoid taking up a static defense; it must be "offensive" in its tactics. It should stay out two or three days, sometimes up to six days, and it should be self-sufficient.

"You must outfox the Jap," this officer explained. "The main point is to confuse him as to what you are doing; then you have an even chance of inflicting casualties. The Japs watch and listen all the time. They attempt all sorts of ruses to deceive our patrols. You can

frequently catch the Jap on the loose – swimming, eating, resting, playing, and so forth. Usually when he is caught under such circumstances, he is absolutely unprotected. Once, during a recent campaign, one of our platoons caught more than 100 Japs completely off guard; the platoon killed 30 of the enemy while the others fled in confusion."

'*The British patrols usually moved by day, and frequently caught the Japs unaware. At night the patrols generally hid out, away from streams, watering places, and trails.'*

In the summer came another move for the Battalion, back into Bengal to Deula; then another, to Bangalore where, on 7 September, Colonel Green, now Officer Commanding, ordered a muster parade. The dramatic news he had for the assembled Jocks was that they were to become Chindits.

Most of them thought they knew what that meant. They'd heard about a man called Wingate and his expedition earlier that year. Being a Chindit seemed to mean marching for weeks on end in the jungle and coming out looking like starved tramps.

One or two there did know the truth exactly, including Jim McNeilly: 'I'd been with the guerrillas for four months on an exercise. There were fourteen of us Black Watch and twenty-eight Gurkhas. All top secret jungle training. We had no idea why, naturally, but they were turning us into jungle instructors. That's what I became. Being in the jungle you have no eyes, you can't see beyond a few feet, so you have to rely on your other senses. If there's a Jap patrol following you, you need to be able to hear it, to hear them talking. Jungle training teaches you to use every possibility, and how to live with rations strictly curtailed. It's a state of mind you have to get into, with your mind being questioned all the time by the jungle's own special noises that you have to learn to recognise, or you'd be a nervous wreck. The other stuff is more straightforward, jungle craft, crossing rivers with livestock, all that.'

Just how straightforward, the Battalion was about to learn. By this time the Cameronians were already learning, including a draft of Black Watch recruits who had 'proceeded overseas' as the army records have it, embarking on 12 March, 1943, at Gourock on the Polish ocean liner MS *Sobieski* . Among that draft, with no idea of where they were going, was my father and an apprentice joiner from Blairgowrie called Fred Patterson. There seems to be no evidence that they knew each other, but they had at least one thing in common; they were both excellent shots.

Fred Patterson: 'Conditions on this ship were like any other trooper, with men packed like sardines. Beds were three tiers high or if you didn't like the company you could always sleep up on deck in the open. Our CO was a Black Watch colonel and the first evening on board he called the Black Watch on parade, all 120 of us, and told us we had the honour of being the ship's U-boat watch.'

The convoy put into Freetown, Sierra Leone, on 27 March and reached Durban on 14 April, where the 120 men camped on a race-course. They stayed for some weeks, keeping fit with forced marches and cross-country runs, before embarking on the SS *Strathaird* on 24 May, destination still unknown. This turned out to be Bombay on 11 June, and thence by train to Deolali, a military town about 100 miles to the north-east which was established in Victorian times but which, according to *Brewer's Dictionary of Phrase and Fable*, lives on in our expression 'doolally', meaning 'bonkers due to locally prevailing circumstances'.

After a few weeks of nothing much happening in the constant rain of the monsoon, volunteers were sought for a new venture called LRP – Long Range Penetration.

Fred Patterson: 'What LRP was we didn't know, but the Black Watch draft were given the order "three paces forward", that is called volunteering, army style, and told to report for medical examination the following day.'

Arriving in Saugor, central India at the end of July, the 120 men found the 1st Battalion Cameronians on a 180-mile jungle-march, and joined in with 100 miles to go. It was still the monsoon but at least they had barracks with hot baths to come back to. Serious jungle training was about to begin.

Fred Patterson: 'We slept on the ground or made beds raised up a few inches to let the rain pass underneath. We lived like animals.'

Chapter Three

Why They Were There

To understand why hundreds of men of two famous Scottish regiments should eventually find themselves wandering for months around a mortally dangerous Burmese jungle, seemingly without purpose and certainly without many other essentials, we need to go back a little in time, to examine two ambitions.

First was the Japanese desire to subjugate the continent of Asia. Second was the compelling urge of a man to prove that he was right.

Of course this is a simplification, but we could simplify it even further. Ask one of the Jocks why he was there, after he'd had an exhausting day's march to nowhere carrying a 70-pound pack, spending his post-rations moments picking leeches from intimate areas of his person, and he would say 'Because Orde Wingate decided this was the best way to stop the Japs'.

We shall try to comprehend General Wingate shortly. The need to stop the Japs is an easier concept.

Japan's short-term objective after Pearl Harbor on 7 December, 1941, was the conquest of the Pacific islands and of Malaya – in particular the British naval base at Singapore. With Malaya went Burma, buffer and possible bridge to India. The British had expected this to be Japanese policy and had planned for it well before war broke out. In the unlikely event of Japanese aggression, the Royal Navy, probably joined by the US Navy, would sail from Singapore, preventing all enemy movement further to the south and taking the war right to the Japanese mainland.

Following Pearl Harbor, the US Navy had its own problems and only three days after that, 10 December, the Royal Navy became the first such force ever to lose a capital ship to aerial attack on the open sea. In fact they lost two, the battleship *Prince of Wales* and the battlecruiser *Repulse*, with 840 men dead against eighteen for the Japanese. The sinking of those two mighty ships turned Singapore from a massive source of wave-ruling power into something it was never meant to be; a defensive fortress. Singapore surrendered on 15 February, 1942.

Meanwhile in Burma, an inadequate mixture of heroic British regulars – including the 1st Battalion of the Cams of course – local troops, other conscripts and one Chinese Division, was failing to hold back an enemy superior in every resource. Rangoon fell on 8 March. Japanese progress to the Burma Road, until then chief supply line from the Allies to Chiang Kai-Shek's Chinese forces, could not be stopped either and the British retreated into India. Burma was gone and, it appeared, nothing could be done about it. India would be next.

One man who had a clear idea about what to do was a British army major, Orde Charles Wingate DSO. His difficulty was that his superiors did not believe in his idea, partly because it sounded mad, and partly because Wingate himself was considered odd. He was not the typical officer even though his father had been an army colonel in India, where Orde Charles was born in 1903.

Returning to England soon after that, he was brought up in a family of Plymouth Brethren, his parents being almost entirely occupied with Christian missionary work. He was made closely familiar with the Bible but not allowed 'normal' books. He was kept away from other boys, educated at home and looked after by two elder sisters, and so grew up devoid of what would now be called social networking skills.

He was sent to boarding school aged twelve where, hardly surprisingly, he struggled to cope. As well as his psychological disadvantages, he was short, with a big nose. He had nothing in common with sporty types. He didn't know how to join in, and his defence was solitary prayer in the school chapel.

There seemed to be few choices open to him for a career. The army was the obvious one, so he took it. Nothing much happened at first in his peacetime Empire duties which were spent largely in the Sudan, but progress could come from his studies of Arabic in the hope of becoming a qualified interpreter. Progress, he felt, was essential. 'I cannot be a nobody,' he said. 'I cannot be a nothing.' He also said he was fated to lead a country.

The change came with a posting to Palestine in 1936 – then ruled by the British as trustee of the League of Nations. Trouble was brewing. The Balfour Declaration of 1919 had envisaged a permanent home for Jews there, but no one had foreseen the rise of the Nazis. The British, Arab, and Jewish leaders had differing viewpoints about a Jewish homeland, but even the Arabs were fairly comfortable with it in the expectation of a general lack of interest among most European Jews. Why would they want to exchange their regular, civilised lives for the hardships and uncertainties of desert farming? A few Zionist pioneers could be absorbed and everyone would rub along. Then the German Jews started pouring in, pushing the Arabs out, and the response was bloody. Arab gangs were going out at night and killing.

Wingate, the devout biblical student, was sent to Palestine as an Arabic-speaking intelligence officer to join officer colleagues who were mainly pro-Arab and anti-Jew. But he saw himself as a kind of herald of the Old Testament; an instrument of government in the Promised Land. The hardy, determined new Children of Israel were to be admired and supported.

For the first time in his life, Wingate had a chance to assert himself. All the better that it should be in opposition to general policy, in rebellion, almost, against the accepted situation which was that Jews were not permitted to fight for themselves; the British would do any defending necessary.

Wingate's idea was to train groups of Jews to form patrols with British soldiers and go out into the country into combat with the Arab gangs, with himself in command. He was wounded and awarded the DSO while doing it, but he took it too far. He became involved politically and so an embarrassment to the British authorities, who banished him from Palestine for ever.

General Archie Wavell had been his CO in 1937: 'His personality was pigeonholed in my mind as that of a leader for unorthodox enterprise, if ever I had need of one.'

This story has nothing to do with Scottish regiments. Neither – except to illustrate his nature – have Wingate's subsequent, and hugely successful, adventures in Abyssinia (Ethiopia), when Wavell's need of a leader for unorthodox enterprise saw him posted, in effect, as officer commanding Emperor Haile Selassie's tiny rebellion forces against the masses of Italian conquerors. Wingate wasn't just willing to try something different; he thought something different was bound to be the answer because those in high authority were incompetent.

Unfortunately for him, nobody seemed to be impressed by his efforts in Abyssinia, the bar to his DSO, or even by his magnificent trickery in getting 10,000 Italians to surrender to his force of one platoon of regulars plus a few hundred tribesmen. Deeply unappreciated, kicked out of Israel, going nowhere in his personal crusade to be a somebody, he cut his own throat. An officer in the next room heard him fall, broke down the door and saved his life.

God had not forsaken Wingate after all and, at last, his achievements with the raggle-taggle irregulars in the Abyssinian desert and in his guerrilla raids in Palestine, somehow percolated upwards and solidified into a reputation. Here was an original, a queer fellow to be sure, but a man who could find ways around and through where orthodoxy could not. Just the chap to send to Burma.

The situation there in 1942 was disheartening to say the least. British soldiers had found the climate and the country entirely alien. There was also the widely held belief that the Jap was by nature more suited to jungle warfare and so suffered less than the westerner in the heat and the flies. He had been specially trained to be a ghost on top of his innate superiority, and he could live on half a banana a day, or whatever it was that grew in the jungle – wild rice maybe – and so needed no supplies.

The British soldier felt he was no match. Wingate disagreed, arguing that the British soldier was more intelligent and more able to learn. Training would make him more than a match, especially when deployed in a revolutionary new stratagem which Wingate called 'long range penetration'. Jungle-trained and jungle-confident troops would reach far behind the front line, supplied from the air. Dropping everything soldiers needed from aircraft had not been tried on any kind of large scale before, and not at all while flying over miles and miles of terrain with no distinguishing features, and many senior people thought it would never work.

In any case, Wingate's arrival more or less coincided with total defeat in Burma and withdrawal of almost all of the last exhausted remnants over the river Chindwin into Assam.

There were no fit men there for him to train and the re-conquest of Burma was an impossible dream.

When General Slim took command of the Fourteenth Army in 1943, he saw straight away that its health and morale were not satisfactory. The sick and wounded were not having the benefit of new drugs and best medical practice. Field hospitals were often too far away from the action, and there was little in the way of air-ambulance facilities to counter that. Discipline and sanitation were not good enough. Preventive measures against malaria in particular were far too lax.

The standard method against malaria was a daily tablet of a synthetic quinine called Mepacrine (US trade name Atabrine). It didn't cure malaria but it did suppress the symptoms. Slim was very keen on it, mounting 'surprise checks of whole units, every man being examined. If the overall result (of the blood tests) was less than 95 per cent positive I sacked the commanding officer. I had to sack only three; by then the rest had got my meaning.'

It took a while but Wingate was able to persuade a few of those in the highest places, including General Slim and the C-in-C Field Marshal Wavell, that his Long Range Penetration Groups (LRPGs) offered hope of some sort. With the temporary rank of Colonel, he was given command of a unit to be formed as the 77th Indian Infantry Brigade, composed of a mixture of Gurkha Rifles, Burma Rifles and various others, and including a battalion of the King's Liverpool Regiment, there for police work and a unit not previously known for assignments like this which was to be called Operation Longcloth.

In training, Wingate led his men through the worst privations. Training, he said, had to replicate operational conditions exactly. Heat, hunger, thirst, mosquitos, leeches and everything else deep in the jungle would have to be endured and ignored. His attitude toward health and medical services were reflections of his pride in his own hardiness.

After seven weeks of hell, the King's Liverpool had almost three quarters of its men on sick parade. Certain measures were taken, including pointing out that passengers could not be accommodated on operations. Being sick would mean being left behind for capture by the unsympathetic Japanese. By the end of the training, hardly anyone was reporting sick.

Wingate later wrote: '*Hypochondria is the prevailing malady of the Englishman and of civilised nations. From earliest youth all are taught to be doctor-minded. National Health Insurance, necessary and beneficial in many ways, plays its part in inducing this disease complex. While a native of India or Africa will not, unless encouraged to do so by a European, even bother to mention a temperature of 103°F, an Englishman will throw himself out of work on account of the slightest deviation from normal. Even common colds are regarded as serious excuses for idleness. To this kind of self-indulgence there is no end.*

'*The first thing that had to be done when training the Long Range Penetration Groups was to root out the prevailing hypochondria. For this, the co-operation of the medical profession was necessary. Although one would suppose my theory to be contrary to their interest, I must admit to having had the full, although sometimes misgiving, co-operation of medical officers.*

'*I am at last getting Platoon Commanders to be their Platoon Physicians for minor ailments and treatment. I never allowed this to interrupt our marches or operations. Gordon said, "A man is either his own physician or a fool at thirty." On this standard a great part of our nation must be classified as fools. I do not sit and take that as an unalterable fact, but set out to alter it, and I hope to succeed in doing so.*'

By January 1943, Wingate had 3,000 men ready to go, arranged in seven marching columns, to leave Imphal as part of a larger attack by orthodox forces. When the larger attack was cancelled, it seemed clear that Wingate should be cancelled too. Anything he might achieve would be short term only: with nothing else going on, the Japanese would simply repair the damage. Men would die for nothing.

Wingate argued on a number of different points. If he couldn't prove the effectiveness of LRPGs now, the influence of non-believers at HQ would be strengthened. His men, moreover, were in peak condition; postponement would mean decline. It was imperative that we learned about Japanese jungle methods, for we knew nothing yet. If we did not attack the Japs, they would be free to attack us as they pleased. And finally, the last enclave of British forces in Burma, the Kachin Levies in the area around the only British-held airfield, at Fort Hertz in the north, would be left to its fate and overwhelmed, with consequent loss of morale among the indigenous peoples.

Somehow Wingate won the day and the game was afoot. It was a very elaborate game, with bluffs, feints, double bluffs and deceptions, including an impersonation of Wingate by an ex-Royal Navy, Royal Irish Fusiliers commando Major, John Jefferies, planting false information in a brigadier's uniform with Jap-sympathising village chiefs. There were no roads into Burma; the only way was up and over the mountain tracks. That done, the 77th Indian Infantry Brigade began crossing the Chindwin on 13 February.

Things went wrong from the start – small things, unforeseen things, such as the ropes being used to pull boats across the river Chindwin sinking to the bottom. The mules, of which there were hundreds, refused to swim and, once cajoled into it, would get halfway over then turn back. Here is a passage from *Wingate's Raiders* by Charles Rolo, based on an eye-witness account:

'The sun rose that morning on a fantastic scene, naked men fighting madly with plunging mules; tiny boats, rocking precariously as shaven-headed little Gurkhas loaded them with precious cargoes of mortars, Bren guns, and rifles; men inflating their rubber dinghies; elephants ploughing majestically through the water, long lines of mules tethered to trees waiting their turn to cross.'

Improvisation and imagination overcame all obstacles. Whatever the chaos, Wingate's subterfuges were sufficient to keep Japanese eyes elsewhere, and his main force crossed the river without being discovered, and with only one man lost; drowned. Even when reports of the incursion reached the Jap high command, the generals could not believe the British were doing anything more than a little reconnoitring.

Two of the columns were directed to the great railway that ran from Rangoon to Myitkyina (with a Jap extension built by POWs to Bangkok via the bridge on the River Kwai). It lay 100 miles beyond the Chindwin and was reached in three weeks, while the other five columns were sent in various directions to find and attack Japanese army units. Supply drops were organised by wireless operated by RAF volunteers, itself an innovation. The drops were mostly successful although representing Wingate's first serious error.

Long-range patrolling was a novelty; long-range rations had not been devised. Without giving sufficient thought to the balance between nutrition and activity, the answer had been simply to multiply the numbers of short-term ration packs to be dropped from the aircraft.

In reality, the provisioning for men expected to march twenty miles a day in jungle heat was no more than living on cheese and biscuits. The cheese came in tins, one for two days. The biscuits were hard tack, as easy to eat as Bonios, so the men usually made a sort of porridge with them, stirring in some of the nuts and raisins they also had. The ration was completed by three tea bags, some sugar and dried milk, a bar of chocolate or other sweets, some salt, and cigarettes.

When Japs were suspected close by, the men couldn't light their fires so it was cold Bonio for supper. As the expedition progressed, air drops became more irregular, so the usual five days' supply might have to be stretched to seven or eight days, or even more. Cut an inadequate day's food by half, while keeping up the work-rate, and deterioration must be expected. Thankfully, some of the marching was surprisingly easy.

Two of the seven columns were ambushed. Mules stampeded, and men scattered according to the dispersal plans they had rehearsed during training. In both cases, some elements managed to join up with other columns. Most of the rest headed back to the Chindwin and the safety of Assam and some wandered far to the north.

The majority kept going largely unmolested, with the Japs still confused about what was happening. Number 3 Column led by Major 'Mad Mike' Calvert of the Royal Engineers, and Number 5 Column led by Major Bernard Fergusson of the Black Watch, found the railway. They blew it up in scores of places, brought avalanches of rock down on it in others, and destroyed several bridges. Where the Japanese interfered, they were beaten off with considerable slaughter to them and small losses to the British. Wingate could have gone home in relative triumph.

He also had the news that his C-in-C, Sir Archibald Wavell, had unexpectedly ordered the formation of another LRPG, to be called 111 Brigade, consisting of the 1st Battalion Cameronians, 2nd Battalion King's Own, and two battalions of Gurkhas, all under the command of Brigadier 'Joe' Lentaigne DSO. This was high-level ratification of Wingate's ideas, although he wouldn't have picked Lentaigne, a fine soldier but not one to take readily to Wingate's unorthodox ideas.

Instead of going home, Wingate devised a new plan. His force could set up a stronghold in the mountains, supplied by air, from which he could make raid after raid, driving the Japs out of the region and setting up a situation where the LRPGs could be relieved by regular troops from Assam. The other possibility was the original Plan A, to cross the Irrawaddy.

After consulting his right-hand men, Calvert and Fergusson, he decided to continue with Plan A, cross a river a mile wide, and harass the Japs some more. Plan A had assumed greater forces attacking elsewhere, with Wingate's men disrupting the enemy response, but those greater forces had never set out. Their mission had been cancelled long ago, as Wingate well knew.

Calvert and Fergusson were what was known in the RAF as 'press-on types', and Wingate was too. He was persuaded, and they pressed on, encouraged by their success so far. They believed that the locals on the other side of the river would be friendlier than they turned out to be. Wingate had been promised this east of the Irrawaddy, but how far east had not been specified. Also, they wanted the experience. Wingate gave the order on 16 March. In any case, two columns operating many miles away were already across.

Again, as at the Chindwin, the force paddled over the river by various means, planned and improvised, without being spotted by the enemy, but that was their last stroke of luck. Supply drops were becoming less reliable; some groups who had lost their radios could not call for supplies at all. The men were flagging. The country was more open, leaving them liable to observation from the air, as indeed soon happened. After believing that their ambush successes had defeated the

British altogether, the Jap generals now heard that their enemies were across the Irrawaddy. Three divisions were sent to correct the situation.

The most urgent concerns for Wingate seemed to be the debilitation of the men, accelerated by lack of supplies and, as Japanese harassment increased daily, there was the problem of what to do with the wounded. The usual procedure was to leave them in friendly villages with payment for their care. This became more and more difficult as the Japanese, knowing the British would be trying to buy food in the villages, occupied them.

Wingate's thoughts turned to retreat; to live to come back in greater strength. Coincidentally, he received orders from HQ to come home right away. He had news from his scouts that the Japs had impounded every boat along that part of the Irrawaddy. He knew what the Japanese commander would be thinking. Wingate's operations had been a deep embarrassment, and the only way a high-ranking Japanese officer could reverse this loss of face was to ensure that none of the British expedition got back over the Chindwin.

A few boats were found from somewhere and some of the men crossed the Irrawaddy, under fire. More crossed over the next few days. With his usual package of diversions and false trails, Wingate's retreat turned out better than it might have, but the sick and wounded had to be left behind, while those who could walk could barely do so.

Wingate and some of his immediate company had to swim the Chindwin to find boats and support for the majority who could not swim. The remains of 7 Column came home via China. Somehow or other, 2,182 of the original 3,000 got back to Assam; to Imphal. A few of the missing lived through the war in POW camps, but most of the 818 missing men were missed for ever. Of the men who returned, only 600 recovered sufficiently from their ordeals to fight again in that war.

Bernard Fergusson spoke later about his experiences on the BBC Home Service:

'We (5 Column) went into Burma in January 318 strong, and came out at the end of April ninety-five strong. Most of our casualties were not so much from enemy action, as from starvation.'

As a defeated sports-team captain would say today, there were positives to be taken from this. They had proved that air support and supply drops could work, and that the Japanese were not so superior in the jungle – which again demonstrated that long-range penetration was a viable stratagem. Even more so, said Wingate, with larger numbers of first-rate troops. Half of the men he'd been allocated were 'the wrong type', but he'd come out with a group of officers who now had the experience to lead better men back in.

Weighing on the other side of the balance was the unarguable fact – at the time – that the operation had not been a military success. The enemy had repaired the railway damage. The Japs had lost more men than Wingate but they could be replaced. Disrupting communications mattered little when no offensive was happening. After the war, it emerged that Wingate's operation had forced a rethink on the Japanese, who had believed that the Chindwin was a reliable moat for their castle. Now they knew that the enemy could and would cross it. Japanese Burma was not as secure as they had thought.

Nobody on the British side had any idea about that, of course. All they saw were three thousand good men marching in soldierly manner, turning into two thousand in a disorganized rabble of half-starved bandits and vagabonds. Staff officers at HQ were contemplating the fall of Wingate with smug glee, but they reckoned without the power of the press.

Amid tidings of early haymaking, the issue of new ration books and identity cards, and the deliberations of the Pacific

War Council in Washington DC, the story broke of Wingate's wreckers. The press embargo was lifted for Friday, 21 May, 1943, and this is *The Times* of that date:

'COMMANDO IN THE JUNGLE
RAIDS INTO BURMA
THREE MONTHS IN ENEMY COUNTRY
From Our Special Correspondent, GHQ, India, May 20

One of the best-kept secrets of the war is disclosed in an official announcement today that a long-range jungle force led by Brigadier Orde Charles Wingate, of Abyssinian fame, and supported entirely by air, has come out of northern Burma after spending three months as wreckers in the midst of this wild, enemy-controlled territory . . . The Wingate Expedition was brilliantly planned and rigorously trained for . . . a glowing story of courage and endurance in troops who were by no means specialists, of bold decisions by an outstanding leader, and a carefully selected band of British officers . . .

. . . Brigadier Wingate, a slight, compelling figure, but looking tired and ill from attacks of malaria and dysentery . . . For him the expedition has proved that unsupported columns can operate in the jungle with the aid of nothing but wireless and air.'

Such invigorating news, coming only a few days after the equally astonishing Dambusters raid (16/17May), did wonders for British morale, civilian and military. Every newspaper was full of it. *The Times* had pictures, one of a crouching Wingate with pointing stick, supposedly 'making final plans for the expedition' and another of some men in their underpants fiddling with a box of tricks beside a river, a 'signal station attached to the column'. These photographs appeared above a modest advertisement offering Bournville Cocoa at 9½d the half pound and regretting 'that Cadbury's Milk Chocolate is not available at present'.

Another ad could have been of interest to Wingate's men. 'Your blood has become sluggish and heavy. You feel off colour and listless. Step out into the Spring with a clear head and a bright eye. Just buy a bottle of Milk of Magnesia today.'

On the following Monday, 24 May, more details emerged. *The Times* again:

> **'JAPANESE JUNGLE TACTICS SURPASSED**
> *. . . an exploit that stands out not so much for the extent of the damage inflicted on the enemy or its impact on the course of the war as for the evidence it provides that a large force supplied from the air can operate for an indefinite period deep in enemy territory without being dependent on orthodox lines of communication.'*

Perhaps *The Times* man had not spoken to many members of the large force, who would have put him right about 'indefinite period', but good news was a rare commodity and Our Special Correspondent made the most of it:

> *'It has shown, moreover, that average British troops, and with them Gurkhas and Indians, can be trained even to surpass Japanese tactics in the jungle and, though broadly such country is best avoided if possible, there is clearly a good deal of jungle fighting ahead before the enemy is driven from the lands he has overrun.*
>
> *'For sheer physical adventure, with a Wellsian blend of modern science, there can never have been anything quite like the Wingate jungle expedition . . . Chindits*

they were called, after the fabulous griffins which guard the Burmese temples, and Brigadier Wingate was the chief Chindit.'

Chindits they were indeed called but only by Wingate at this point. Much to his irritation, he already knew that the griffins were *chinthé*, the word for lion. He wanted lions, and 'chindit' sounded right to him so, regardless of linguistic exactitude, that was the word he decided on. It was a term nobody else had used, not even the men themselves, and *The Times* had picked it up from Friday's *Daily Express* or perhaps from conversation among reporters in Imphal, as a name Wingate had coined back in February, before setting out. Anyway, as well as chief Chindit, Wingate had other titles foisted on him by imaginative journalists. In the *Daily Mail* he was 'Clive of Burma'. *The Times* reported he was also known as the 'Lord Protector of the Pagodas by the friendly Burmese villagers, to whom he wrote a manifesto speaking of the "mysterious men who have come among you, who can summon great air power, and who will rid you of the fierce, scowling Japanese".' The mysterious men included experienced commando regulars, 'but for the most part they were married men from the north of England, aged between 28 and 35, who would normally be called second-line troops, and had come out to India to do internal security work.'

This presumably refers to the men of the King's Liverpool Regiment:

'For months Brigadier Wingate trained them in jungle warfare, river crossing, and long, forced marches with heavy packs, until they were determined shock troops, ready for anything . . . many came out comparing the relative values as food of elephant, mules, horses, snakes, banana leaves, and roots.'

Our Special Correspondent was having a whale of time writing this, the longest article in the paper that day, and he could not resist the British tendency to make light, afterwards, of an experience both bloody and awful. He put together a note on Major Calvert, 'altogether a rather legendary figure (who) had nine fights and killed any number of Japanese', with Major Fergusson's tales of eating raw water buffalo and using the pages of a Trollope novel as cigarette papers. Finally:

> *'They crept up one night to a village and saw four Japanese soldiers sitting round a fire as it might be round a bridge table. "I lost all my fear of the Japanese then," said Major Fergusson, who described the look of absolute terror on their faces. He threw a grenade in the middle of the fire and that was the end of them.'*

This was a real incident, occurring in the village of Hintha on the way back from the Irrawaddy. Fergusson recalled that, in the lead of his column, he approached not realising at first that the men were Japanese. When he did, he lobbed a grenade into the fire and the four of them fell back in synchronised death as if they had rehearsed it.

A later *Times* editorial commented:

> *'The remarkable success of the wrecking columns led by Brigadier Wingate . . . has shown what opportunities lie before mobile columns of individually trained troops working in close liaison with an efficient and enterprising air force. Such troops may not be able to hold invaded territory; that, after all, is not their function. But their power to divert hostile forces and to disrupt hostile communications might be of immense value were they cooperating with a more formal invasion.'*

As we shall see, such wisdom as could be found in 'The Thunderer's' offices was absent from the places where it would be needed most. Even so, if the Jock in the jungle in 1944 did wonder why he was there, these newspaper reports were a large part of the reason.

At the time, Wingate himself made no effort to capitalise on the venture in terms of media coverage, despite his anxious desire to set up another, bigger expedition. The niceties of PR were lost on him. While reporters from around the globe combed the camps of Imphal for stories, Wingate stayed in a hotel room in Delhi, plotting how he might convince the high command with his own arguments, rather than employing the pressures of public opinion. The man from the *Daily Express*, William Burchett, tried to interview Wingate but was instead treated to a literary discussion between the brigadier, lying naked on his bed, and Major Fergusson on the merits or otherwise of a recent book about Emily Brontë.

Wingate's priority at this stage was his report. It would be full and frank, and tactful only where the behaviour of his brother officers was concerned.

Not only did he fail to understand the value of publicity; he also had no idea about diplomacy. If he was going to recruit the senior officers at India GHQ to his cause, he would have to do things their way. If he had ever heard the expression 'softly, softly, catchee monkey' he must surely have thought it applied only to trapping wildlife because, instead of submitting his report respectfully to GHQ for approval, he published it in printed form and sent it to all and sundry, including a government minister, the Secretary of State for India, L. S. Amery.

GHQ's reaction was swift. The Chief of General Staff ordered the report's withdrawal until it could be appraised and – perhaps – approved after due consideration, consultation etc., etc. Wingate was distraught. Those at GHQ were masters of delay. Any chance of another expedition before the next monsoon was disappearing into a dozen pending trays.

Help, once again, came from the fourth estate, that body of scribblers whom Wingate so disregarded. Just as the report was taken from the public domain, so the embargo on Chindit photographs was lifted. On 7 July every British newspaper had pictures of exhausted heroes with beards, and dressed in rags and bush hats. The Chindits were front page news all over again.

At the Carlton picture theatre, Bing Crosby, Dorothy Lamour and Bob Hope were appearing in *Road to Zanzibar*. At the Windmill Theatre, in *Revudeville* (165th Edition), there were continuous daily performances from 12.15pm to 9.30pm, in which 'the whole company of Windmill Girls and Revudebelles are seen at their most typical in their finale on board a pirate ship', but what thrilled and excited the nation was pictures of smiling if rather emaciated and very hairy men:

'NO RAZORS – *A typical bearded member of the Wingate expedition – razors were deemed an unnecessary luxury – and Major Fergusson, a column commander, wearing a monocle which was dropped for him by parachute.*'

'A DARING EXPEDITION – *These pictures were taken on the remarkable wrecking expedition led by Brigadier Wingate which penetrated over 1,000 miles into the wild, enemy-controlled jungle of northern Burma.*'

(A little journalistic licence there; many of them had marched something like 1,000 miles, maybe more, to penetrate by 200 miles or so.)

There was Wingate, bushy beard, belligerent eyes and his

new trademark – the classic colonial hat, the pith helmet – apparently much too large for him.

Whatever they thought at GHQ, it no longer mattered. Letters of interest and congratulation came in from the King, the Viceroy designate (Wavell) and Mr Amery, and the timing was perfect. The Americans were putting pressure on the British to be more active against the Japanese; Amery wrote to Churchill with Wingate's report; Churchill wrote to his personal military advisor and forces go-between, General Sir Hastings Ismay:

'All the Commanders on the spot (in the Indian Army HQ) seem to be competing with one another to magnify their demands and the obstacles they have to overcome . . . I consider Wingate should command the army against Burma. He is a man of genius and audacity and has rightly been discerned by all eyes as a figure quite above the ordinary level. The expression "The Clive of Burma" has already gained currency. There is no doubt that, in the welter of inefficiency and lassitude which have characterised our operations on the India front, this man, his force and his achievements, stand out, and no mere question of seniority must obstruct the advance of real personalities to their proper stations in war. He . . . should come home for discussions here at an early date.'

The summons came. It was non-specific in detail and Wingate left Delhi on 30 July, arriving in Blighty on 4 August to be directed to an appointment with the Chief of the Imperial General Staff, Sir Alan Brooke. This meeting went well, with Wingate explaining that his next, much larger expedition, would need the best of everything, including first-rate troops from front-line regiments. Sir Alan listened sympathetically, promised favourable action, and told Wingate to report to 10 Downing Street.

The Prime Minister was to leave next day for Quebec, from Glasgow on the *Queen Mary*, to meet President Roosevelt with all the most senior Allied commanders. He wrote:

'I was about to dine alone . . . when the news that (Wingate) had arrived by air and was actually in the house was brought to me. I immediately asked him to join me at dinner. We had not talked for half an hour before I felt myself in the presence of a man of the highest quality. He plunged at once into his theme of how the Japanese could be mastered by long range penetration groups landed by air behind enemy lines. This interested me greatly . . . I decided at once to take him with me on the voyage.'

Churchill was well known for doing business over the dining table. He once told Montgomery that if he could have dinner once a week with Stalin there would be no problems at all. So now here he was, taking a relatively junior officer, who had started the war in charge of an anti-aircraft battery in London, across the Atlantic to meet the President of the USA.

On board, Churchill sent for Wingate and proposed a meeting with the chiefs of staff where the brigadier could present his ideas. It went down well, with Wingate describing a plan involving six brigades and, this time, the finest troops. In Quebec, disagreement with the Americans was foreseen on many points, European and Far Eastern, and this is what happened, except everyone was enthusiastic about Wingate's plan. He met Roosevelt and made a private presentation to the President, Churchill and Lord Mountbatten, describing his intentions of flying troops in by glider, who would set up three strongholds well behind Jap lines and, supplied from the air, would launch assaults on enemy positions and communications.

It is not known exactly what stirring words he used to his eminent audience, but later he wrote down what he meant by 'stronghold' in terms which certainly stirred enthusiasm in those already well disposed:

> *'The ideal situation for a Stronghold is the centre of a circle of 30 miles radius of closely wooded and very broken country, only passable to pack transport owing to great natural obstacles, and capable only of slow improvement. This centre should ideally consist of a level upland with a cleared strip for Dakotas, a separate supply-dropping area, taxi-ways to the Stronghold, a neighbouring friendly village or two, and an inexhaustible and uncontaminatable water supply within the Stronghold. The motto of the Stronghold is No Surrender.'*

The President, the Prime Minister and the noble Lord were thoroughly convinced. Telegrams were sent to India giving top priority to the LRPGs.

These messages were received with fury by the staff officers at India GHQ. The new C-in-C, Sir Claude Auchinleck (Wavell had been made Viceroy), was a moderate on the subject of Chindits, but the rest of them were violently opposed. All manner of military objections and counter-arguments were put forward, and long lists were prepared of reasons why not.

Regardless of the amount of truth and good sense in Auchinleck's response, he and his officers did not know that the decision was now a political one. The British could not back down on their only major point of agreement with the

Americans. It was the one thing everybody wanted and so, whatever Auchinleck and his generals might say, Wingate was going to get his 26,500 Chindits and GHQ had better get used to the idea.

Furthermore, the new South East Asia Command would have Mountbatten at its head, a great admirer of Wingate, and General Arnold, commander of the USAAF, had promised what amounted to a private air force for Wingate's exclusive use.

From an office in London, Wingate set about organising his great expedition. He needed men – 'the best only' – and equipment, and he could order pretty well what he liked. For air support he would have a task force created and commanded by a famous fighting man, Colonel Philip Cochran, who at first thought Wingate to be some sort of caricature of an upper-crust limey with an impenetrable accent and a pedagogic approach. Cochran was soon converted, like so many men of action:

'I suddenly realised that, with his radio direction, Wingate used his guerrilla columns in the same way that fighter-control headquarters directs planes out on a mission. I saw it as an adaptation of air to jungle, an application of radio-controlled air-war tactics to a walking war in the trees and the weeds . . . When I left him, I was beginning to assimilate some of the flame of this guy Wingate.' (As reported by the American broadcaster Lowell Thomas.)

The flame of the guy smouldered on route to India, quenched briefly and impatiently on the way by the water in a flower vase as he waited without refreshment for his next flight. He was sure that he was going to meet opposition by inertia from the top brass at GHQ, and he was right. In Delhi he found he had no accommodation made ready, for him personally or for his work. There was no office, no secretary, no staff car, and no use of the aircraft he'd been promised. At his first conference with his opponents, as he saw them, all the heads of department and other senior officers were intent on objecting to every element of the Chindit plan and, it appeared, equally intent on putting this upstart in his place. Only eighteen months before he had been Major Wingate. Now he was Major General Wingate (acting), a junior whippersnapper telling his betters what to do.

Without Churchill's backing he would certainly have seen his scheme disappear into a paper mountain of army bureaucracy. Even with that personal direct line to the very top, he was frustrated at every turn. He went scouting for training grounds. When he returned to Delhi, he still had no office, no car, no staff. Well, Mountbatten was coming soon. He would sort things out.

Somehow, Wingate's invitation to Mountbatten's ceremonial arrival was not sent, but he went anyway despite feeling very ill indeed. Mountbatten saw him, spoke, said he wanted to discuss Chindit matters as soon as possible. Soon was not possible; Wingate had some kind of typhoid fever, caught almost certainly from his flower-vase water, and he only just managed to survive it.

By the end of November 1943 he was more or less well again and back to his almost daily necessity of knocking down walls of opposition and walking through them. By the beginning of December, the basic organisation was complete and the men were in training in Gwalior, central India. Special Force, as it was now known, was around 24,000 strong in seven brigades, including the American brigade which, as the time approached, would be switched away from Wingate to earn its own fame, fighting with the Chinese under General Frank Merrill as Merrill's Marauders.

Number 14 Brigade, commanded by Major Thomas Brodie DSO, acting Brigadier, comprised battalions of the Bedfordshire and Hertfordshire Regiment, the Royal

Leicestershires, the Yorks and Lancs, and the 2nd Battalion of the Black Watch. Each battalion was formed into two columns of 400 men or so, mostly infantry platoons with rifles and light machine guns, but also including a heavy weapons party – mortars, anti-tank and machine guns – and a specialist unit for demolitions and tricks such as booby traps. A reconnaissance section was bolstered with Burma Rifles men, and there were other specialists for aircraft liaison, engineers' work, signalling, medical, and muleteers. A standard column had around sixty mules with a man assigned to each one.

This animal was unknown in India – they mostly came from South America – and was certainly unknown to the soldiers of the Black Watch, except they'd heard the expression 'as stubborn as a mule' and would soon learn the truth of it.

Bernard Fergusson on the BBC Home Service: 'The muleteers had the worst job of the lot. They had to take care of the mule's load as well as their own, and make sure that the mules' backs didn't get as sore as their own backs did.'

Chapter Four

Never Seen Anything Like It

Major David Rose DSO: 'Wingate told me I was to command one of two columns in the Chindit Force. I told him I had no jungle experience. He said that I would be attached for fourteen days to some Chindits already in training. I would soon learn, and then I'd have time to train my own men.'

That was pure Wingate. He chose his men, and he knew he had chosen well.

David Rose: 'All the officers of the Chindits were assembled to hear Wingate's exposition of his strategy for bringing the Japanese attack on India to a standstill, how we would construct a chain of fortresses astride the enemy's lines of communication. Each fortress was at first to be supplied by air drops but very quickly landing strips would be made for re-supply and evacuation of casualties. To invest and attack these forts would require far more men than their defence, and as each attack was mounted, the Japanese would be ambushed and harried by mobile columns of Chindits. Later, we would plant vegetables to help spin out our rations.'

Wingate's first campaign had done little to tone down his gospel, but it convinced him that his notion of medical self-sufficiency had been impossibly idealistic. All of them who were there, Wingate included, had been deeply disturbed by having to leave sick and wounded men behind. The second expedition could not go ahead without a proper plan for evacuation, and aircraft had to be the answer. Marching columns would only be burdened by their ailing colleagues for short periods, and the strongholds would not be turned into field hospitals. Those not sick enough for the air would have to keep going and recover as they went along.

The training to implement this strategy began for the Black Watch in early October in central India, at Jhansi, on the Uttar Pradesh side of the border with Rajasthan, where it was winter: cool nights but warm days and no rain as the monsoon had finished. The Cameronians, with their Black Watch contingent, were already well into their training.

Fred Patterson: 'During October our anti-malarial pills ran out and within a few days we had every hospital for miles full of malarial patients. Malaria is a very weakening disease but our high standard of fitness helped us through.'

They went to other locations too – Saugor, Rajgarh, Lalitpur – but all in the same region, until mid-March. Much time was spent crossing and re-crossing the rivers such as the Betwa in Madhya Pradesh, and the Ken, where there is now the Panna National Park. People spend holidays there having elephant rides, boat trips, and jungle safaris in the hope of seeing a tiger.

'Ken river with its fresh, clear water, flows through the ravines of the Vindhya range and sustains the varied wildlife including the crocodile and the gharial,' says the tourist information. A gharial is another sort of crocodile.

In the words of the commander of 77 Brigade, Mike Calvert, training consisted of weeks of 'marching, watermanship, mules, air supply, jungle shooting, air support with live bombs, digging, column marching, column bivouac, patrols, Royal Engineer signals exercises, medical and veterinary tests' – blood, sweat and tears in other words, conditioned by the lessons gained in the first expedition. A very few of the men, some of the Burma Rifles for instance, had seen it before because they'd been on that first attempt, and a few, like Corporal Jim McNeilly, had taken the instructors' course, but for most it was an entirely new experience. More than that, it was the first experience of real soldiering for a lot of them – those new recruits who hadn't been to Somaliland or marched on the Burma retreat.

Even for men who had seen action, this was trial by ordeal. There also had to be a change of attitude. Mostly, British soldiers thought that in some ways fighting the Germans was fighting their equals. Only a few of the Germans were genuine Nazis. The rest were just blokes like us. You'd give a wounded German a cigarette and a drink of tea. But a wounded Jap, he'd shoot you in the back while you were fetching his cup. So shoot him first, and make sure he was dead. Prisoners could not be accommodated on LRPGs anyway, so forget all that stuff about chivalry. This was a different kind of war.

Brigadier Barclay, after the event, would put the same point more subtly:

'Unwounded (Japanese) prisoners were unknown, and a wounded man would fight on to the last. If deprived of arms they would bite and kick in their efforts to inflict injury. This had one advantage; it made it unnecessary to guard, and evacuate, large batches of prisoners – which would have been a very real embarrassment under such conditions.'

The challenge for the Jocks was to turn themselves into jungle fighters as good as the Japanese. They had a few short months to become Chindits. Regulars, or new boys just shipped out from Scotland, all of them were ordinary men; men from the towns and villages who'd taken the King's shilling in their country's peril.

David Rose: 'We were certainly not supermen. We were not volunteers and we hadn't passed any fitness tests. We had no idea about growing our own food, much less killing it. Who was going to deal with a bullock, and cut it up to share out? Have we any ex-butchers in the column? Anybody here know how to cook without pots and pans?'

Front-line troops they most definitely were, but they were not your super-selected special-forces types, your SAS and SBS volunteers – at least, not yet. But, it was a special-forces job they were supposed to do and that is what they were called, Special Force.

The Cameronians Battalion was to provide two columns, named from the old regimental numbers, 26 and 90, and likewise, the Black Watch. Under Rose was 42 Column, which was 400 men from B and D Companies, parts of HQ Company, a platoon of Burma Rifles and various specialists including the medics, signals and air force liaison. The animals, sixty mules, a few horses to carry wounded men, and some bullocks, would fulfil a dual role. Under Lieutenant Colonel Green was 73 Column, which was A and C Companies plus the same extras.

Of huge importance were the Burma Rifles for reconnaissance. They were mostly anti-Jap Burmese, men generally referred to as 'Burrifs', originally short for Burma Rifles but a term applied to all the sympathetic locals and guides whether officially Burma Rifles or not.

Some were of the Karen people, a Baptist Christian minority in Burma, and others were Kachin, tribesmen from the hills with a fearsome reputation but likewise largely Christian. The Kachins had never been under direct British rule but were governed through a system of client clan chiefs and, like the Karens, were (and still are) a national minority, with their own language and culture. As the British brought colonial law and order, so the position of peoples like the Karens and Kachins equalised, but such reforms were reversed by the Japanese and their sympathisers, the Burma Independence Army (BIA), which had helped the Japs invade.

The BIA grew into quite a force, attracted various renegade gangs, turned on the Karens and Kachins and encouraged hostility to British troops among the local populace, spying on British army movements and giving false information. The Japanese formed a new Burma National Army in 1943 and gave a kind of notional independence to the country, but the reality was continuous and brutal Japanese military rule, with the BNA doing a lot of the dirty work. Later, almost all the population turned against their Jap overlords, but that hadn't yet happened when the Chindits were operating.

The Scots Battalions still had their pipers with them. In Rajgarh, the officers of 73 Column decided to have a Burns Night.

Bill Lark: 'Our commanders had got themselves in with the tea planters up there, and they wanted to put on a show. They had to instruct the local cooks in the matter of how to make haggis, and of course I had to pipe it in. When that was all over, there was a pile of haggis left so I took it down to the lads who very soon saw to it. And it wasn't a bad try at a haggis, not bad at all. I don't know what they had in it. You don't ask questions like that, but it tasted all right, and it was different from our usual food. Maybe it's a traditional dish up there now.

'Anyway, they came to the pipe band and said they were desperate for muleteers, or you can go to duty (be normal infantrymen) if you want to. We didn't know one end of a mule from the other but we all decided to be muleteers. We were each assigned a mule, which we had to get to know, and we had to sit on our mule while the veterinary cut the voice box out. We couldn't take any chances on any hee-hawing in the jungle. So we learned to water them and feed them, saddle them, put the loads on properly, and clean their feet every night with a little hook. Mine was the medical mule, Katina, named after the woman on Crete who used to do our washing. Katie, we called her. She had no white marks, which is the white hair that grows again from a saddle sore.'

Major Desmond Whyte, DSO, was the senior MO with 111 Brigade. He was interviewed for Imperial War Museum records in 1992:

'We started training with six doctors (in the brigade). The training was quite strenuous, physically and psychologically, and we lost a lot of our otherwise excellent young doctors (because) they couldn't stand it. They had to give up. It was the knowledge of what you were being led into. You had to be your own surgeon, your own physician, dermatologist, everything medical, your own eye surgeon, et cetera et cetera, orthopaedics. You were on your own. Nobody to turn to except your orderlies.

'(For equipment per column) we were allowed one pannier; one side of a mule, for medicines, dressings and instruments, which were utilitarian rather, and that pannier was never big enough.'

After the war, the US Army Medical Department compiled a comprehensive set of reports on military medicine in India and Burma. Here is an extract from their deliberations on the Chindits, written mostly by the man put in charge of medical matters with the campaign already underway, the interestingly named British General W.J.Officer, a colonel at the time:

'*The medical establishment of Special Force was under ranked and undermanned. It consisted of (1) a Deputy Director of Medical Services and the Headquarters medical section of three officers and four other ranks; (2) the brigade medical units, each composed of two medical officers, a warrant officer, and twenty other ranks; and (3) the column medical units. Wingate intervened to prevent the senior medical officer from attaining a rank commensurate with his position as D.D.M.S. Wingate also reduced the size of the column medical detachments below the level which the medical administration believed would be adequate.*

'General Wingate suggested that use could be made of the Column Padre as a medical orderly but this was not agreed to by the D.D.M.S. However, after more discussion, it was finally decided by the General that the Column establishment would be one Medical Officer, one Sergeant and two other ranks R.A.M.C. on the columns with Padres, and one Medical Officer, one Sergeant and three other ranks R.A.M.C. on columns without Padres.'

Although this arrangement was approved by GHQ, the Deputy Director never agreed to it. He was over-ruled and, as he had repeatedly forecast, it would prove quite inadequate. When platoons went out on their own, taking a medical orderly with them, resources would be too thin elsewhere. When there was no medical orderly with a group out on a task, the responsibility for casualties would transfer to the senior military officer, whose knowledge of first aid was sketchy to say the least. All the officers went on a first-aid course before going in, but with little time and the soldier's usual lack of interest in medical matters, expectations of benefits were not high.

Extract from Colonel Officer's medical report:

'An "Air Base Set" of medical supplies was designed as a standard 3-month reserve for each brigade. Field experience revealed that the set was severely understocked in the drugs used to treat diarrhoea and dysentery, foot diseases, and helminthic worm infestations. The special

medical panniers and haversacks which the columns
carried soon needed replacement. None were available
and improvised substitutes had to be hurriedly produced.
(helminthic – intestinal)
   'Bandages must (in future) be coloured green or khaki.
On more than one occasion a white bandage has been
made the target of a sniper's bullet and has been the
direct cause of more than one man's death.'

Bill Lark: 'We took our mules into the river Ken and swam them around, and went on marches together. Mules are hard-working and hardy, but they're not pets. They don't start off trusting you and being docile. You have to build a relation-ship, and some of them can be stroppy. Very stroppy.

'Anyway, the muleteers were each given a Sten gun. The rest of the boys had rifles, much heavier, and there was one Bren gun per section. And we trained to get used to K rations, although you never could get used to them.'

The emergency K rations were American, designed to be used for short periods only. The Chindits would exist on them for months. Basic and frugal though they were, at least they were an improvement on the cheese and biscuits given to the first expedition. Standard issue was fifteen packets; three a day for five days. The breakfast packet, for example, as officially described in its US version, contained a tinned meat product, biscuits, a compressed cereal bar, soluble coffee, a fruit bar, chewing gum, sugar tablets, three ciga-rettes, water-purification tablets, three sheets of lavatory paper, a can opener and a wooden spoon. Dinner and supper were very similar but without the lavatory paper. Dinner had a canned cheese product, biscuits, a candy bar, gum, bouillon powder, sugar, salt tablets, cigarettes and matches. The supper packet had meat again, rather than cheese.

The biscuits, beverages, sugar, fruit bar and so on, were packaged in a laminated cellophane bag while the canned-meat and cheese products were put in a chipboard sleeve-type box. The two units were assembled and sealed in a waxed carton enclosed in the non-waxed outer carton labelled with the K ration design and colour.

The Chindit version seems to have been packed without the chewing gum and water purification tablets.

As Bill Lark remembered it: 'You got a packet in a wax wrapper, about nine inches long and four and a half wide, and in it there was a little tin of some kind of meat. According to what it said on the tin there were various different sorts, but they were all just slight variations on Spam. Then there was a little thing of sugar, and two or three biscuits, and a chocolate bar or a squashed up fruit sort of bar, and three cigarettes. And a coffee sachet.

'We used to crumple up the waxy cardboard and set fire to it. You held your tin mug over the top and got your water a bit warm that way, with your coffee powder. Then you dunked your milk bag, which was powder in a muslin bag supplied separately, in and out. It went into a lump, so you could give it a little squeeze and save it for next time. One of your three daily packets had soup powder instead of coffee, like you'd use an Oxo cube now. You never got any tea, except occasionally in the supply drop the lads back at base would put some in. Really it was just snacks. Not filling.'

Or, as another Chindit put it: 'We had two conditions – one in which we felt unfed, the other in which we were unfed.'

Many of the men developed cravings for the simple things of life, like buttered toast, a boiled egg, apple pie or, in times without water, the idea of a cold beer. The thought that such were freely available at home was enough to drive a man near to madness.

Colonel Officer:

'*Rations suitable for our particular type of warfare are not yet available and will not become so before the beginning of the next campaigning season. If it had not been for the K-type ration, the modern (British) ration would have differed in no way from that of the last war. While there is no doubt that the importance of a good ration for the fighting soldier has been appreciated for more than a century – commencing with the world famous Napoleonic dictum – little effort has been made by those responsible to implement this. It has been left to the Medical Services to introduce nutritional experts on to the staffs of Armies in an attempt to stimulate interest and research in this important subject.*

'*For this type of warfare certain principles in the provision of a diet are indisputable and absolutely essential. First, it must be light in weight and of reasonable size and shape. It must be packed in one-man, one-meal units. It must be calorifically sufficient, well-balanced, and must contain a full complement of vitamins. Lastly, it must be made in a sufficient number of variants to avoid monotony.*

'*The importance of a sufficient diet with the necessary variability to stimulate interest in its consumption cannot be overemphasised and there is no doubt whatsoever that diet in itself has an enormous effect on morale.*

'*American K type ration is without doubt the best that has been produced yet, and though monotonous, is less so than any of the other types, for it does make some attempt at variety, which none of the others do.*

'*Every opportunity for giving a change should be seized, and whenever a column gets into a stronghold a ration other than the one upon which it has been living should be sent in at once. Amongst the articles of this, pickles, sauces, etc., must be prominent.'*

Note that this was written after the event. No Jock, in a stronghold or otherwise, had recollections of pickles, sauces etc. Occasionally, the standard air drop of K boxes would have British extras with it. Corned beef came in a new form, at pouring consistency. Tinned fruit in syrup was a delight but it did nothing good for the digestive system. Sometimes there was an issue of rum. Sometimes there would be the British 'compo ration', designed for groups of men up to fourteen, and which came in large tins and packets; the contents to be shared. The tins were too heavy to carry, so the men tended to eat for tomorrow and the next day when such food was around, and it was the treat of treats when they could heat up some of the famous Maconochie stew. This delicacy, familiar to members of all the British armed forces including POWs in receipt of Red Cross parcels, was made by Maconochie Brothers, contractors to the War Office and suppliers of rations – tinned meat and vegetables – during the Boer War and onwards. The statement on the label, 'The meat in this tin is prepared in its natural juices', caused much discussion.

Excerpt from a post-expedition report:

'**Malnutrition. Approximately 1 month after their withdrawal from Burma, 34 cases of deficiency in the vitamin B complex had been admitted to hospital, seven cases from 14 Brigade, the remaining 27 being distributed between 77 and 111 Brigades. All cases occurred among B.O.R.s (British Other Ranks, as opposed to officers, Gurkhas, West Africans, Burrifs).**

'**Of the seven patients admitted from 14 Brigade, all suffered from multiple neuritis. A previous history of**

69

malaria was volunteered in six cases, and three had suffered from jungle sores.

'It is of interest to note that the neuritis did not develop until almost 1 month after the substitution of Compo and later the Rehabilitation, scales of rations. It is difficult to assess whether the above indications of malnutrition in these personnel of 14 Brigade were due to complications appearing after malaria, or were the sequelae of postdiphtheritic ulcerations. It is considered more likely, however, that the manifestations were occasioned by the bodily reserves of vitamin B becoming depleted during the lengthy period of existence on K rations, and the failure of the later diets to replace it in sufficient quantity.

'Although the discovery of these cases of avitaminosis would seem to indicate that the vitamin content of the K ration is deficient, this is in fact not so, and those cases of avitaminosis which did occur, can only be attributed to the well-known fact that the men threw away or failed to eat some vitamin-containing part of the ration. While this cannot be condoned it can never be avoided, and it does indicate the absolute necessity of the inclusion in the ration of a separate multi-vite tablet.'

Of the twenty-seven severe malnutrition cases from 111 and 77 Brigades, most had symptoms of lassitude, muscular weakness and anorexia.

'One of the most striking manifestations was the extreme degree of mental depreciation in these patients. Lassitude and, in some cases, even inability to move was marked. Depression was severe, and orientation and concentration were also affected.'

David Rose: 'Roosevelt and Churchill knew nothing about jungle warfare, and the general staff knew about the same amount. My friend Bernard Fergusson had been on the first Chindit operation and he told me what to expect. The most important thing of all was to prevent disease, particularly malaria. Fever and marching cannot go together. We had a pill to take every day, and any man who didn't take it was in effect condemning himself, because he would become a casualty, and casualties could well get left behind. Part of the problem was the talk about the pill making you impotent. Nonsense, but men will believe nonsense.'

Extract from Colonel Officer's medical report:

'Tabs Mepacrine Hydrochlor were always available in sufficient quantities from 16 Indian Depot Medical Stores, but the issue to columns was perhaps the most difficult problem encountered by the Brigade Medical Unit. Some brigades endeavoured to include tablets in ration drops, whereas others left it to column medical officers to indent for their requirements, but both of these methods led to a great deal of duplication in issues and still reports were received that suppressive Mepacrine was not being received by the columns.

'Assuming that many men in the Force would contract malaria, the Force could survive only if its men took daily doses (0.1 gram tablets) of Mepacrine. Fergusson reports an occasion when one of the columns exhausted its supply for a short period of time. A notable upsurge of malaria cases followed soon afterward. However, the massive breakout of malaria in the Force occurred late in the campaign, when deficiencies in the supply of Mepacrine were unlikely.'

As Fergusson himself wrote later:

'In one respect we had the wrong attitude to malaria: we looked on it as inevitable; we believed that we were all bound to get it every so often. Good work and propaganda by commanders, doctors, officers and men elsewhere has shown that this is by no means true. But in one respect we had the right attitude, in that we never treated malaria as a disease meriting evacuation.'

David Rose: 'I think we quite enjoyed the training. We were a team, even the mules, doing it all against time. And there was the air support. We had never imagined having our own bombers on call. Ordinary life, though, was very basic to say the least. There were no privileges for officers, not like on the first trip. I heard about one officer on that who rode on his horse most of the time and kept a luxury bedroll by his saddle. Oh no. Everybody ate the same food, carried the same loads, slept on the same bare ground with one blanket each. Any extras in the supply drops were shared out. Anybody not pulling his weight was letting the side down.' (Note: not every column was as punctilious about social equality as Major Rose's.)

Bill Lark: 'Nobody told us anything about feeding off our surroundings, what we could eat and what we couldn't, or if there was anything there to eat at all. There was no training on how to live off the jungle. I mean, who was there to train us? We only had our own officers and they were as daft as we were.'

The matter was still to be resolved of how to get so many thousands of men into the Burmese jungle, behind enemy lines, quickly, in secret. Some would march in, some would fly in, and the idea of gliders came up for discussion. It looked good; a Dakota could pull two gliders, one on a short rope and one on a long.

David Rose: 'We were in the Indian jungle, on a training

72

march, when I had a signal from HQ to expect a VIP visit at such-and-such a map reference, noon tomorrow. It was General Wingate, brought to us by truck. Strange man. The troops worshipped him, but I didn't. He was a brilliant strategist but thought everyone was like himself, without limits of performance, and he would take no advice from anyone on anything. When he was making his plans, he forgot that the pins on his maps were human beings. Anyway, he stood there in his sola topee, leaning on a long stick, and told me some American air force gliders had turned up and we needed to find out how to use them. We needed to learn about loading unwilling animals, and bulldozers and whatnot for building airstrips. There was no mention of the actual flying part, which in fact would prove to be the real problem as far as I was concerned.'

Wingate wanted volunteers, so Major Rose was one, and a group of his Jocks would be the others. Volunteering would mean an interlude in the forced marches, so gliding it would be.

The glider was the Waco CG-4A, which the British called 'Hadrian', just short of 50ft long with wingspan over 80ft. It could carry fifteen men including the pilot. Other common loads were: small truck or jeep with radio equipment and driver; two men with loaded trailer; light artillery piece, ammunition and crew; small earth-mover and driver; or anything that weighed about 4,000lb which, in our case, would include livestock.

It had a blunt nose section which swung upwards, so cargo could be loaded straight in to the body, and quickly out. Fully loaded, gross weight was around 7,500lb, with maximum tow speed 150mph, although slower was better and more usual.

To say that gliders turned up was somewhat lacking in detail. They came in crates, and took a while to put together, then they had to be tested for airworthiness. Such delays were not always built in to army schedules.

We must not forget the pilots. They were crash-landing on purpose, often behind enemy lines, often knowing that their first mission would be their only mission. Usually there was a plan for getting back, requiring their gliders to be picked up from the ground, but otherwise the pilots might become infantry soldiers whose knowledge of flying was suddenly irrelevant.

General William Westmoreland put it thus: 'Every landing was a genuine do-or-die situation for the glider pilots. It was their awesome responsibility to repeatedly risk their lives by landing heavily laden aircraft containing combat soldiers and equipment in unfamiliar fields deep within enemy-held territory, often in total darkness. They were the only aviators during World War II who had no motors, no parachutes, and no second chances.'

Besides the well known saying about stubbornness, mules are also proverbial for their kicks, and first-hand acquaintance with the truth of that soon came as the soldiers tried to persuade these beasts into the gliders. Kicking holes in the fuselage didn't even need full power, and the ponies and bullocks also joined in the excitement and showed it in the usual tail-lifting way. Slipping and sliding about in piles of manure plus holes in the aircraft would lead to the use of crates in future. The earth-moving machinery, on the other hand, was simple to dismantle into manageable sizes.

David Rose: 'The first trial was to be in daylight, and that went all right, and so did the night-time one except – I thought at the time – for my glider. We took off from a little airstrip called Sorga, heading for a flare path in the jungle that had been cleared of trees by blowing them up. My glider didn't come down according to the book. Apparently – we were learning fast – the moment to free the glider from its towline, called pulling the plug, is highly critical in its timing. The

74

Dakota just chugs along and the glider pilot decides. Our pilot missed it and so couldn't get down in the proper place.

'The first we knew about it was him shouting "Lift your feet, lift your feet", as he aimed us between two trees so the wings could take some of the force of the crash, which they did. We were all a bit shaken but not hurt, and we clambered out to find that we were only a couple of hundred yards or so from where Mountbatten and his staff were standing, watching the fun. We made our way over and I was presented to the great man and he said "Everything all right, Rose?" and I said "Not quite, sir, but we've no casualties." Which was the best I could think of at the time.'

Rose soon learned the 'not quite' applied to one other glider, not among those which had made successful landings:

'We'd been in a pair with Captain Dalrymple, Hew Dalrymple, my second in command, and they hadn't arrived. Mountbatten said he'd been told everyone else was here, so what was I going to do about it. I said I'd get a Dakota to hook us up in one of the good gliders and I'd go back to Sorga by the same route and look for fires on the way, which Dalrymple would have lit to attract our attention if he'd crashed somewhere. "Good idea, good idea," said Mountbatten, "do that," and off he went.

'The technique was that a Dakota flew over with a hook on the end of a nylon rope, and tried to catch the glider which had a construction on it like a set of rugby posts where the hook was supposed to attach on the crossbar, as it were, which was a cable. I collected whoever was unlucky enough to be near me, which was the RSM, the MO, the padre and one or two others, and we sat in the glider in great expectation.'

The Dakota flew over the glider but nothing happened. It flew over again; still nothing.

'I asked our pilot if this happened often. He said no, it had never happened as far as he knew, but then it was the first time they'd tried it with men on board. They'd only ever done it with sacks of sand before. The third time it caught us and we shot up at the most extraordinary rate.'

The pick-up rope, just under an inch in diameter, was only about 200ft long, as opposed to the standard tow rope length of 350ft, so they were in a kind of express lift.

'We then settled into calm flight and everybody kept a lookout, but we could see no sign of Dalrymple's fires in the black jungle below. We reached our little airstrip at Sorga and cut, and circled and landed, and I went over to the hut in quite a state, already composing letters to next of kin, and there were Hew and his chaps playing cards.

'I should have been delighted but I was furious, and asked him what the hell he was doing there, and it turned out that our first glider had had another narrow escape that we didn't even know about. As we'd left Sorga, his tow rope had become crossed with ours, and Dalrymple's glider pilot had seen this and cut them free, otherwise all three of us would have gone down. They'd landed and, well, that was our rehearsal to prove to Mountbatten that we could do it.'

Training was coming to an end and it was almost time to put it to the test.

Bill Lark: 'We had very good boots, green leather from South Africa, and when they were new I tied mine together and left them in a stream overnight. Next day we were off on a route march so I put them on wet, and when we got back they fitted me. We had a second pair which had to go in the store, so they could be flown in when we needed them, and I decided I'd put my pipes in the store as well. I wrapped them up in anything I could find, towels and cardigans the lads were throwing away because they couldn't be taken into the jungle, and fitted my parcel into a kitbag and gave it to the Quartermaster Sergeant, Jackson. I'd been denied playing my pipes at Tobruk, so I said to Jackson, when we need pipes in this jungle, they're here.'

Meanwhile, Orde Wingate had been having a great deal of bother. A conference called Sextant (the Quebec one had been Quadrant) was held in Cairo in November 1943, concluding on 26 November. Churchill, Roosevelt, Chiang Kai-Shek and Mountbatten discussed the war in the east with their military leaders and a seven-point plan was agreed, of which one point was Wingate's LRPGs. The other six were all orthodox operations to capture places and advance on different fronts, resulting in the liberation of upper Burma before the 1944 monsoon, and the retaking of the whole country after that.

Churchill and Roosevelt went on to another meeting, with Stalin in Tehran. Stalin pressed for the opening of the second front, that is, the invasion of France that would become D-Day, 'Operation Overlord', in June 1944. Roosevelt was keen to support the Russians. The British, with limited resources, could not do everything and be everywhere, so for Churchill it became a rather invidious choice: China or Russia, Chiang Kai-Shek or Stalin. He had to go with Stalin. Forces, particularly amphibious forces, would have to be withdrawn from the seven-point eastern plan and be reallocated in the west, to Overlord.

Chiang Kai-Shek felt betrayed – as he had been – and reacted by withdrawing his promises too. The seven-point plan was down to its last three: the LRPGs and two modified, conservative advances meant only to shore things up rather than conquer Burma.

Wingate came to know about most of this but not all, and so did his detractors at GHQ. It seemed to the chief Chindit that history had repeated itself. Just as his first expedition had been left high and dry by cancellations and reallocations, so the same was happening now. Without the concerted efforts elsewhere, what would be the purpose of LRPG 1944?

In any case, as the year turned and with time pressing hard, Wingate was still without mules and aircraft, and none of the equipment he had ordered months before had arrived. He still had Mountbatten and Churchill on his side, so he took a gamble. He wrote to Mountbatten, basically telling him that it was no good anyone, not even him, the Supreme Commander, issuing orders for Chindit support. The opponents, the senior officers of the Indian Army, would do nothing, as they had been all along.

Wingate also wrote to GHQ, accusing them of deliberately not implementing policy, and offering his resignation.

Mountbatten's reaction was positive, to say the least. 'Wingate has been promised certain things and while I am here I will see that he gets them. I want no more arguments on the subject.'

The resignation offer was forgotten but there were still many enemies, as Wingate saw them, whose opinions ranged from 'Wingate is a jumped-up nobody who must be taught a lesson' (that was everyone, according to Wingate), to those who genuinely believed the Chindit operation to be doomed, and doomed on a massive scale.

Wingate also saw the dangers of an operation meant to support other, bigger incursions when those incursions were not going to happen, so he amended his plan. The Japanese were, he was sure, planning an invasion of Assam. He would redefine the objective as one of attack and disruption. He would establish strongholds behind Jap lines, which would then be garrisoned by non-Chindit battalions. Thus secured and supplied, the Chindits could mount offensives of their own.

At a meeting in Ranchi with General Slim, the modified plan was agreed. Slim then went back on it, removing the proposed garrisons. Wingate offered his resignation again. Then a compromise was reached with a much-reduced commitment to garrison the strongholds, but with more forces promised conditional on Chindit success. As Wingate could not imagine anything other than success, he found this acceptable, with the overall strategic requirement as before; cutting the supply lines going north to the Japanese facing Stilwell, creating confusion and wreaking havoc generally, and thus making Chinese and American victory more likely.

Chapter Five

Orders To Proceed

Operation Thursday was due to begin in early March. A full month before that, the first Chindit incursion set out from Ledo in north-east Assam, starting point of the great Ledo Road being built by the Americans and Chinese, under General 'Vinegar Joe' Stilwell. This road, such a complex and difficult project that Churchill believed the need for it would have disappeared by the time it was finished, was meant to replace the airlift to Chiang Kai-Shek's forces over the Himalayas (called the Hump), made necessary by the Jap occupation of Burma's roads and railways.

Under the command of Bernard Fergusson, 16 Brigade was to march from Ledo over the Patkai Hills (Patkai Bum), across the Chindwin and on down to Indaw, where the airfields would be siezed. Wingate would then have fully-functioning, ready-made landing grounds for other troops. Progress was slower than expected, beginning with seventy miles of mud and rain, leading them to the Patkai range, an outpost of the eastern Himalayas – not as high as Everest and K2 but still presenting a tremendous obstacle to foot soldiers with much of the highlands over 4,000ft and peaks reaching 12,000ft.

Extract from Fergusson's report: .

'The march was the heaviest imaginable. The rain was torrential and almost continuous. No single stretch of

level going existed between Tagap and Hkalak, and few thereafter.'

Fergusson on the BBC Home Service: 'None of the tracks were wide enough to allow two men to walk side by side, so we had the ludicrous business of four thousand men, and seven hundred animals, strung out 65 miles from end to end.'

It was 35 miles to Hkalak, with bivouacs at 5,000ft, leeches, flies and lost supply drops. At one point, the going became impossible for the mules, so the men carried their loads for them. Those 35 miles took nine days.

Meanwhile, 77 and 111 Brigades were completing their training and preparing for their launch into country north-east of Indaw. They would be flown in to a location as yet unspecified. The three divisions of 15 Corps, attempting by conventional army methods to take the port of Maungdaw in the Arakan, had been surrounded and were fighting for their lives, relying on air support to sustain them, which of course meant that resources were spread ever more thinly.

Fergusson and 16 Brigade were scheduled by Wingate to cross the river Chindwin on 16 February. They didn't reach it until the 28th. Wingate flew to see them on 1 March, as the crossing was about to begin, taking with him four journalists. Presumably, with a newly awakened sense of the value of PR, this was with future copy in mind as the operation was top secret. Extract from *CBI (China-Burma-India) Roundup*, an American forces newspaper printed in India, dated March 9 1944:

'BURMA – *Several columns of 14th Army troops, organized on the lines of Wingate's expedition a year ago, have crossed the upper reaches of the Chindwin River and have taken the Jap by surprise. Secrecy of the movement prohibits the publication of details so far.'*

The British press was limited to a fairly non-committal release, to be published on 16 March. *The Times* and the rest had to keep to generalities:

> *'Today's announcement by the South East Asia Command shows that the Burma front is in a lively state of eruption from one end to the other, but news from the northern sector, where columns of the Fourteenth Army have crossed the River Chindwin in support of General Stilwell's Chinese and American forces, is scanty.'*

The American papers at the time were criticising the British, in the person of their supreme commander, Lord Mountbatten. The United Press Agency declared that high American military authorities were 'displeased and concerned' over Mountbatten's failure to launch a significant Burma offensive, especially as the monsoon season was near, which would mean a halt to all activity for six months. Mountbatten was described as a 'good man' hampered by his having to depend on 'the British-Indian military system for his requirements'. Merrill's Marauders had had their first success much trumpeted, but that wasn't a conquest of Burma.

Training at the Dukhwan dam on the river Betwa, like the Ken a tributary of the Yamuna, the Cameronians were surprised by a visit from Wingate a few days before they were due to move to Assam. There was a parade of the men with no officers present, and Wingate spoke. Captain Geoffrey Straight is quoted by Philip Chinnery: ' . . . whatever he said, the men subsequently appeared to be both inspired and impressed.'

To put this in context, the men in question had just completed a solid month's real-life exercise on nothing but K rations. Wingate must have been an inspirational speaker indeed, and perhaps the incident accounts for the very high esteem in which Wingate was held by my father. On the other hand, we have the recollection of Fred Patterson:

'We had a pep talk from Lord Louis Mountbatten, followed by a talk of a different nature from General Wingate. "You are soon going into Burma to do what you have been trained for and if any of you come back out, you haven't done your job." That was how his message came over to us. He looked like a madman, bearded, thin-faced, sunken eyes. He looked down at my mate and me and said to an officer, "What are these?" as if we had crawled out of the ground.

'Various punishments were outlined, thirty-six lashes with a rope for stealing rations, and so on, and we were not allowed henceforth to write home. A card would be sent to our nearest and dearest, saying that due to the nature of operations, we were unable to write. By the time I could write home again, more than six months later, my parents had had two cards.'

The next men to go in under Operation Thursday were the reconstituted 77th Indian Infantry Brigade, commanded by Brigadier 'Mad Mike' Calvert DSO, and 111th Indian Infantry Brigade, commanded by Brigadier 'Joe' Lentaigne. Initially they were nineteen columns plus support, including the three of 111 under the separate command of Colonel 'Jumbo' Morris, called Morris Force. They were to go in by glider, landing on two forest clearings codenamed Broadway and Piccadilly.

Colonel Cochran, an airman ignoring a landsman's orders, had secretly taken reconnaissance photos of the landing grounds. There had been a slight possibility that the Japs would notice such unusual activity, which was why Wingate had forbidden it. Against that were the photos for all to see, showing Piccadilly covered in neatly arranged tree trunks. This revelation came in the afternoon of 5 March, on the airfield at Lalaghat; they were supposed to fly that night. Nobody had any real idea of why these logs should have appeared – it was later discovered to be normal Burmese forestry practice, laying them out to dry in the open – but there were no logs on Broadway so it was decided to take everyone there, necessarily more slowly.

The first of the first included Americans with equipment to build an airstrip for powered aircraft. Their glider, like all the others, was loaded to the limit and beyond, and each towing plane had two. There were no tree trunks to wreck the landings but forestry practices did for them just the same, with deep furrows made by elephants dragging logs across the clearing when the ground was wet.

Gliders damaged on landing could not be cleared away, so other gliders crashed into them, or crashed trying to avoid them. Some were recalled while in the air, and more force-landed elsewhere after tow ropes broke. It looked like disaster. Calvert sent the signal 'Soya Link' – codename for failure and the most derided dish in the canteen. Just over half of the intended first wave had arrived, thirty-seven gliders, with more than sixty men killed or wounded, including some of the American engineers, the remainder of whom nevertheless began work on their airstrip in the dark.

Came the dawn, and matters did not seem so bad. Calvert could count 500 fit men and mountains of supplies, and an airstrip soon to be completed, all 200 miles behind enemy lines and the enemy had no clue they were there. He sent the signal for success, the antonym of tofu, 'Pork Sausage'.

During the first day, every casualty was flown out by light aircraft. Wingate's first campaign had convinced him that hypochondria was not diagnosed after being hit by a Jap bullet. He and all his men had been profoundly affected by leaving behind their sick and wounded. A well organised airlift had been deemed essential for the second expedition.

Between 16 September 1942 and 13 March 1943, when he sailed for India, the writer's father, 14254229 Thorburn A. D, was Black Watch in training and is here, fourth from left, back row, as part of the boxing team.

Just arrived in India, June 1943, these Black Watch boys had not the slightest idea of what they were in for.

Drafted from the Black Watch to train with the Cameronians in the Indian jungle, Andrew Douglas Thorburn is pictured here probably in August 1943 when he was briefly a Lance Corporal, unpaid. Soon after, he went down with malaria for the first time. The rule was you lost your field rank and extra pay while off sick, which seems rather mean as he was unpaid anyway.

He went sick again on 10 October, which coincides with the malaria pills running out (see page 60), but was back in the jungle with the column on 14 November. Come February 1944, he was restored to Lance Corporal, paid this time.

Frederick Charles Patterson, in the same Black Watch to Cameronians draft, on leave at Jubbulpore, 30 December 1943. He also had been in hospital with malaria when the pills ran out but looks quite chipper, perhaps because it was Hogmanay the next day. Supplies of Irish whiskey and Cape brandy were obtained from a Mr Wazir Ali of Jubbulpore market, followed by an open-air snooze, missing the actual moment of the new year entirely.

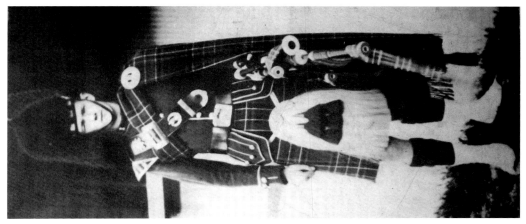

Piper William Lark was a Black Watch regular from before the war, serving in Palestine, Somaliland, Libya, Syria and Crete before becoming a Chindit. When in full fig as here, on official duty, those with the rank of Piper wore the Royal Stuart tartan rather than the regimental, which was worn by the drummers and Drum Major.

Some of the Black Watch/Cameronian draft in India before the training got serious.

Piper Lark in his ceremonial kilt, the NCOs and others of C Company, Second Battalion Black Watch, pose for the press in the noonday sun.

Orde Charles Wingate was a complex figure with revolutionary ideas and an unshakeable faith in himself as great military strategist and soldier of the Lord. He was tireless, able to drive himself beyond endurance. Perhaps his chief fault lay in his inability to understand that most men are not like that.

With a musket, fife and drum . . . the pipe band of the Second Battalion, The Black Watch, pictured in Ranchi, India, in 1943.

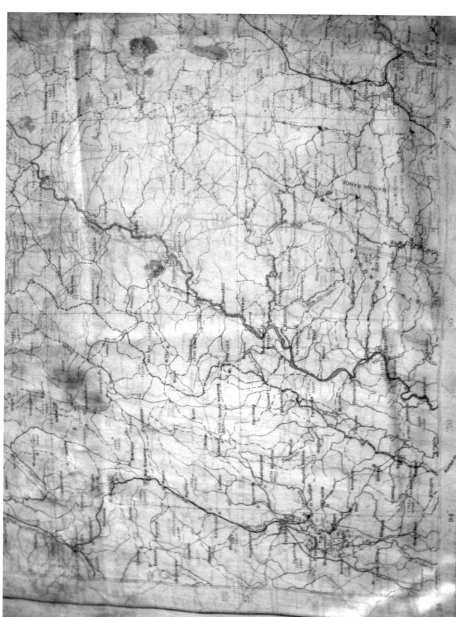

Every Chindit was issued with a map of Burma, printed on both sides of a square yard of orange silk. This was universally known as the panic map, because it was meant to help soldiers, individually or in groups, who became lost and cut off from their fellows, to find their way back to India and safety. Bearing in mind the small scale of the map, the widespread lack of map-reading ability and the featureless nature of monsoon jungle, Jim McNeilly's advice, to find a river and follow it upstream to China, would probably have been of greater use.

This section of the map shows the western part of Burma, the border with India and the two hundred miles over which the 1944 Chindits flew in. The 1943 Chindits walked in and, somehow, mostly struggled out over the same territory, including crossing the river Chindwin (centre of map) both ways.

Our photograph is of the very map carried by Fred Patterson and has some stains from his sweat. A practical application of the maps was to knot them together to make a signal banner for waving at passing aircraft.

This section of Fred's map shows the 1944 Chindit battleground. The Irrawaddy runs down centre right from Myitkyina. Indaw is bottom left, with the great railway running up to Mogaung, and the Mesa river runs down the left side. The Indawgyi lake is upper left, west of Pinhaw. The landing ground and stronghold of Broadway was more or less dead centre, east of Mohnyin by the Kaukkwe Chaung. White City was just to the west of the railway above Mawlu, and Aberdeen a little to the north of that. Chowringhee is off the map to the south, below Ngno.

The 1943 expedition marched well off our map to the right/east, over the Irrawaddy and as far as Mangla and beyond.

The lions that guard the Buddhist temples of Burma are called Chinthe (pronounced tchin-thay, 'th' as in them). It is thought that this association with guardian lions, rather than with the name of the river Chindwin, resulted in the word Chindit for members of Special Force. Such 'branding' caused much irritation among the India GHQ staff officers who attempted to ban its use in newspaper reports.

The Waco CG-4A glider, which the British called Hadrian, was about 50 feet long with wingspan over 80 feet. It could carry fifteen men including the pilot or the equivalent weight, approx. 4,000 lb, in kit, men and animals. The nose swung up to allow loading straight in to the body and quickly out.

The gliders came to Special Force in crates, presumably with instructions, and had to be assembled at high speed and tested for airworthiness.

Wading across a chaung, elephants first, with a few locals on hand with rafts to help out, many of these men are suffering from dysentery, which is why they are doing without trousers. The picture is from the first expedition in 1943 but it stands for all of the Chindits, most of the time.

The Chindits' undeniable triumph was to prove the great value of two technical innovations in ground warfare – battle directions and supply demands by wireless, and supply demands met from the air (*see* photo next page, top). Long range penetration could not have happened without.

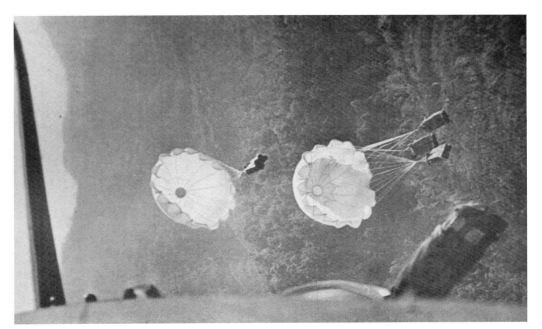

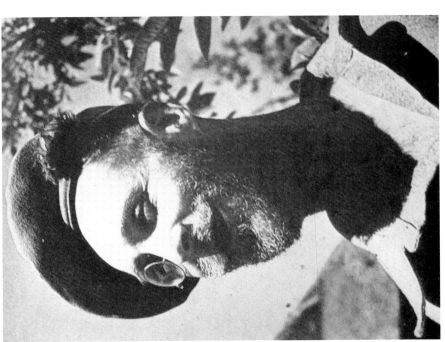

Black Watch officer Bernard Fergusson, otherwise Baron Ballantrae of Aucharne and of the Bay of Islands, KT, GCMG, GCVO, DSO, OBE, last of the British-born governors of New Zealand, commanded a column on the first Chindit expedition as Major, and 16 Brigade on the second as Brigadier, marching all the way from Ledo to Indaw and part of the way back again. His was probably the most famous monocle in the British army, which is to say any armed force anywhere. Legend relates that he had to have monocles air-dropped with the rations, although it is not explained how he came to lose the ones he took with him.

(Right) General Wingate as his men saw him, with his sola topee and his long bamboo stick.

Medical category A: Able to march, see to shoot, hear well and stand active service conditions. Subcategory A1: Fit for dispatching overseas, as regards physical and mental health, and training.

Medical category C: Free from serious organic diseases, able to stand service in garrisons at home. Subcategory C1: Able to march 5 miles, see to shoot with glasses, and hear well.

Doctor's report after amoebic dysentery: 'Your liver will last you ten years.'

Part II Order	Postings	Offr's Inits.	Part II Order	Postings	Offr's Inits.	Part II Order	Postings	Promotions	Offr's Inits.
14/42	58 P.T.N. 6.8.42		1/27/43	X (11) 10.10.43		Ind 1/34/43		Unpaid A/Cpl 26-8-43	
39/42	H'8. I.T.C. Black.		1/5/44	1 Bn 14.11.43		1/24/43		Rfn (X II) 29. 8. 43.	
	Welch 16-9-42			X II		1/53/44		U/e (C/el) 3.2.44	
			1/16/44	1 Bn 3.2.44		"		Rfn X (ii) 20.3.44	
ITC. 259/42	10'd Bn. 30.12.42	A.10.	1/53/44	X (ii) 20.3.44					
			1/21/44	X 44 22.4.44					
10/40/43 Draft RNG A.O. 13.3.43			msg/Base R X 75/44 X II 22.5.44.						
RO Bom BAY	B.R.C. Bombay		office 42/44 Emb. for M.E. 29/44						
12/43	11. 6. 43		5/ RO/202/44 Y.List A. 9.9.44.						
7 st WAMS	Cameronian								
20/43	1st BN. 31/7/43	c/f							
Ind 12/43	X (II) 29-8-43								
1/36/43	1 Bn 24-9-43								

Entry Date			Dates on which Amendment Slips were sent to Central Card Index	
1 9 AUG	2 5 SEP 1942		18 OCT 1944 (19)	
	6.49515	M 80459 9	19 MAR 1945 (12)	
	94 25 JUN 1943	-9.12.43 4		
		1 SEP 1944 (19)		

The X II or x (ii) code stands for withdrawal beyond RAP (Regimental Aid Post) to field hospital. In training, malaria cases would be hospitalised; in action, you were expected to march on. Here we see Rifleman Thorburn was sent to hospital on 29 August 1943, returned to training 27 September, re-hospitalised 10 October, and back in training 14 November.

Promotion to paid lance corporal came on February 3, with hospital again on 20 March, two weeks after flying in to Burma. Whether he was injured in the landing or had contracted the amoebic dysentery that finished his soldiering, we don't know, but he seems to have gone back in and out again before being finally classified as non-effective on 22 May and shipped home, 29 July.

The Stinson Sentinel L5, nicknamed the Flying Jeep for its versatility, needed only 375 feet to take off and much the same to land at less than 50 mph. Made of steel tubing covered in fabric, it could take a lot of punishment and was easily fixed in the field. The ambulance version could take one stretcher case, loaded through a door at the back of the aircraft; a second wounded man could go in the co-pilot/observer's seat, behind the pilot, if the plane was flown solo. The L stood for liaison, and this was one of the 'grasshopper' types also represented by the L4 Piper Cub. Pilots liked the L5 in the jungle because it could provide a very rapid rate of descent, which made it perfectly suited for getting into short fields, some of them pretty rough, or 'unimproved forward airstrips' as they were technically known.

The Japanese paper money, thoughtfully styled in English for the benefit of Burmese used to that language, was missing several elements normally found on promissary notes, including the promise itself to pay the bearer. Also there was no serial number, and the Chief Cashier of the Japanese Government had neglected to sign. Little wonder that the locals much preferred the solid metal of rupee coins to such perishable and dubious currency, printed as an early example of quantitative easing.

In this detail from the silk panic map, you can see Hopin, down centre, on the Burma railway. Blackpool was just to the north-west of there, in the hills above. The Indawgyi lake is to the west, and north-east is Taungni, which was Stilwell's next target for 111 Brigade and the Cameronians after they were forced to abandon Blackpool.

At Jubbulpore, October 1943, Fred Patterson (right), who made it through Blackpool, and his pal Duncan McKerchar, who did not.

"Forgotten Men" Of The Far East War

Amazing Jungle Exploits Of Black Watch Heroes

HERE, told for the first time, exclusively in the "Sunday Mail," is the story of some of the " forgotten men " in the Japanese theatre of war—the story of heroic men of the Black Watch. The exploits of these "Scottish Chindits" in the steaming jungles of Burma have not, perhaps, received the attention they deserve because of the other drama unfolding nearer home across the English Channel.

The men of this Black Watch battalion have been fighting with Major-General Lentaigne's 3rd Indian Division (the Chindits), under General Stilwell's command in the Mogaung Valley.

The stories of the men you will read about here were told specially for the "Sunday Mail" to an official observer as the columns of this force were in bivouac in Mogaung Valley.

Courage, ingenuity and resource are the watchwords of these men of the Black Watch in their fight against the cunning yellow men.

A Black Watch corporal probably owes his life to a packet of "K" rations, but not in the normal way, for he never ate them, Cpl. S. Drummond, of 6 Charles Terrace, Gargunnock, Stirlingshire, was leading his section during a night attack on a hill feature near Karwan.

Cpl. Drummond

Beside his water bottle he had strapped a " K " ration packet. Not until the action was over and he had come through a hail of Jap fire did he disover that a bullet had shattered the packet, deflecting its flight.

" I had to do without my breakfast that morning," said Drummond to the "Sunday Mail" observer.

Listen, then to the story of Corporal A. Stenhouse, of Chapel Place, North Queensferry, Fife. Corporal Stenhouse has vowed he will not shave his head again when he goes into action against the Japs.

A close crop nearly cost him his life in an ambush south of Napin village.

Stenhouse's section Bren gunner, Pte. Bernard Saxton, of Doncaster, mistook him for a Jap during the confusion of a stand-to alarm. Dull rumbles and crashing through the jungle led the Black Watch men to believe the Japs were coming in on a night attack. In the scramble to positions, Saxton fell on his gun. The barrel locking nut came out and the whole thing fell to pieces, leaving the barrel in his hand.

At this moment, Saxton saw a figure crawling towards him only a few feet away in the jungle undergrowth. As the figure came nearer, he saw the shaven head of a typical Jap. He said to himself "Well, here goes, it's him or me" and was just going to smash in the Jap's skull with his Bren barrel when he recognised his section corporal.

The cause of the alarm, a herd of bullocks, had stumbled into the Black Watch bivouac. Fortunately, no one opened fire in the confusion and the position was not given away to the enemy, who some ten minutes later put in their appearance.

The Scots could hardly believe their eyes, for at the head of the marching Japs, was an officer riding a huge white charger which stood out y even by night.

Pte. W. M'Greary, of Inverkeithing, Fife, said all hell was let loose. M'Greary himself crowned the Jap officer's shout with burst from his Bren at five yards range. It blew the Jap's head right off, but his white horse dashed off into the jungle

(Further Black Watch exploits will be published in our next issue.)

The Scottish *Sunday Mail* reports the Black Watch ambush on the track near Napin, with a third candidate offered as the man who shot the Jap officer from his white charger.

After the bayonet charge at Labu, the success of which was credited to Bill Lark's bagpipes, the Black Watch were flown out. Piper Lark was painted in the safety of India, somewhat recovered from his six-month jungle march, by artist S. J. Ivey.

HOSPITAL SHIP "ORANJE"

The *Oranje* was the fastest ocean liner of her time, with a top speed of 26 knots. She was making her maiden voyage to the Dutch East Indies when the Germans invaded the Netherlands and ordered the captain to come home. Instead he sailed to Australia and offered her as a hospital ship. She also served as a troop ship with the Royal Australian Navy, and in peace time made the Southampton-Sydney run many times, carrying immigrants, the so-called £10 Poms. On her voyage from the Middle East to Liverpool in September 1944, she was carrying a great many very sick soldiers, including Rifleman Thorburn.

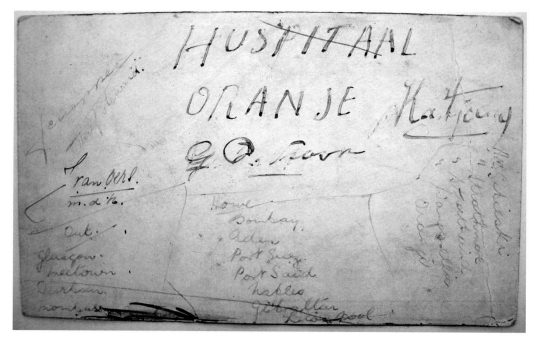

In pencil on the back of the *Oranje* postcard are listed the ships that transported the Black Watch-Cameronians draft to India, including Fred Patterson and Andy Thorburn: MS *Sobieski*, SS *Strathmore* and SS *Strathaird*. Coming home was on two Australian hospital ships: the *Wanganella* from Bombay and the *Oranje*, via Aden, Port Suez, Port Said, Naples and Gibraltar.

Cameronians pipes and drums at the fort, Delhi, February 1945.

Thus would the columns not be burdened by the lame, and the strongholds would not become hospitals. Needless to say, those with ordinary ailments would cure themselves on the march.

Fred Patterson: 'We had trained for nine months and now we were quiet, stepping into the unknown, flying into Burma in the dark, and the sight that met our eyes was unbelievable. It was like a proper civilian airport, only the landing was a bit rough.'

By night, another 900 men came by Dakota. By 11 March, the whole of 77 and 111 Brigades with all their animals and kit, were in at Broadway and at a reserve landing ground called Chowringhee, where some of 111 had gone, 50 miles away from the rest and on the wrong side of the Irrawaddy.

Fred Patterson: 'We disembarked on the edge of the jungle and took up defensive positions to allow the mules time to get off and loaded up, then marched two or three miles away from the airfield and made harbour for the night. We awakened on the morning of 12 March with the sudden realisation that we were now 200 miles inside hostile territory.'

Broadway had been reconstituted as a garrisoned stronghold, and still the Japs knew nothing. They had found the nine gliders cut loose and lost on their side of the Chindwin during the first night and killed most of the occupants (a few did get back) but, for the moment, they could only speculate about the purpose.

Calvert set off for the railway with 77 Brigade; Morris, from Chowringhee, headed for the Chinese border and the northerly section of the Burma road. Lentaigne, also in Chowringhee with the majority of 111 Brigade, had the Irrawaddy to cross before he could join up with his Cameronians and his other Battalion of the King's Own Royals currently at Broadway. The Cameronians' first task was to march westerly, about 100 miles, to block a road running from Nankan to Banmauk, which meant crossing the main road and railway line above Indaw, the Mesa River, and another important road, the Indaw-Banmauk. Scheduled arrival at the concentration point, near Dayu, was 19 March. They didn't get there until 22 March, Jap activity having forced them to divert from their planned route.

Fred Patterson and his Black Watch mates were with 26 Column:

'Six days after landing we had a road and a river to cross, 300 yards wide and knee deep, which was all right for me as I couldn't swim. Our recce platoon didn't do too good a job, so we were crossing a few hundred yards downstream of a Jap camp at breakfast time. Some of them were in the river, bathing.'

In the ensuing fight, one Cameronian rifleman and two mules were wounded, but, 'Worst of all was our RAF officer. He took a bullet in the small of his back which came out high in the chest. He had to spend the next three or four days on horseback before we could find a place to make an airstrip to fly him out.'

The Cams set about their roadblock as they had been ordered to do, and were on the point of implementing when new orders came to move north-west to the area between Indaw and the border town of Tamu. Although this was not a region blessed with much in the way of highways, there were byways that the Japs were expected to use as they built their threat towards India. The Battalion's two columns operated separately here for three weeks, harassing, demolishing, and ambushing.

Coming to a road, an ambush was laid for the next passing vehicles. One came along and was dealt with, but the firing stirred up a great deal of trouble. Again, there was a Jap camp nearby.

Fred Patterson: 'Before darkness fell we watched Japs drive

up in hordes and take up position across the valley. Three-inch shells were soon hitting us, and there was a cry like a football crowd cheering a goal as the Japs swarmed over the valley floor like ants.'

The enemy were beaten back, with mortars and machine guns, and the expected second attack didn't come. Men were dead, including two of Patterson's platoon, but many more on the Jap side. It was decided not to hang about. After the burial parties had done their work, the Column moved out in darkness, not something they often did, and there was very little sleep that night.

At about this time, the Second Battalion of the Black Watch left training base for Monachera in Assam, 15 March 1944.

War Diary: '*March 21, after travelling by train and paddle steamer, 73 Column consisting of A and C Companies, elements of HQ Coy, 1 Platoon of Burma Rifles and attached RA and RE personnel, under the command of Lt. Col. G. G. Green arrived at Monachera in the early afternoon. 42 Col, B and D Coys plus as above, under the command of Major Rose DSO, arrived before dark of the same day.*'

The journey was described by Jim McNeilly: 'We hadn't known where we were going until we got on the train. We were in ordinary carriages for four days, very cramped it was, and we got to the Brahmaputra River and all piled out. The officers said we needed a march to loosen ourselves up, so we had one, and when we got back the carriages were gone and all they had for us was flat carts – railway, you understand, not horse-drawn. So we were arranged on these carts for maximum comfort and we had another day of that.'

'We were there (Monachera) overnight, and next day seemed normal enough. Come evening time, and we had our mess tins open and were away to have our tea, then suddenly everybody was rushing about. We just left our tea, scrapped it altogether, and ran to get our kit. That was all the notice we had, and we still didn't know we were going in to Burma. Not till we got to the aerodrome.'

Or, as the regimental diary put it: *'Orders were received late in the evening for the two Cols to proceed into Burma.'*

News of Japanese movements made a major attack on Assam, and Imphal in particular, seem imminent. It would have occurred to Wingate that his remaining jungle-ready troops might be recruited to conventional defensive positions. Better to send them into Burma before the same thought occurred to the general staff.

David Rose: 'As it happened, we weren't flown in by glider, despite all our rehearsals. We went in by Dakota.'

War Diary: *'March 23, 73 Col reached Lalaghat airfield and were to be flown in Dakota aircraft of USAAF during the afternoon to Aberdeen (codenamed airstrip/stronghold, established by Fergusson and 16 Brigade on their way to Indaw), which is one mile north of the village of Manthon. It was found that the aircraft couldn't take the full load predicted because of the short-ness of the runway, and so 1,000lb was removed from each, which meant they went out on two separate days. Some aircraft didn't find Aberdeen and returned to base. First impressions of Burma were pleasant – two heavily wooded ranges of hills running along together, the village striking also, being well built of teak and bamboo and each house on stilts. Villagers put in an appearance and the Burrifs were soon bargaining for poultry etc.'*

Bill Lark: 'We flew from Assam in an American Dakota. I was in charge, being a corporal, and there was us men and five animals, three mules and two ponies, in frames built inside the aircraft, and one parachute. This American pilot came back to see if we were all right, and I said, "Look, there's only one parachute". So he just shrugged and said that was the only one they had.'

War Diary: '*March 24, the rest of 73 and part of 42 were flown in to Aberdeen. Major General Orde Wingate arrived in a Mitchell (North American B25 medium bomber) and met senior officers. As he was leaving for Lalaghat he congratulated the men on being the first Scottish troops to arrive at a Scottish airport in Burma. He and a considerable party of people were killed in an air crash (unexplained).*'

This account differs from others, which state that Wingate left his Mitchell at Broadway and flew to Aberdeen in another aircraft, which then took him back to Broadway.

From there he went to Imphal, where he met Air Marshal John Baldwin who had written to him, suggesting that the proposed move of Chindit HQ from Imphal to Sylhet put it too far from RAF and USAAF centres. Sylhet, by now, was a fait accompli, so they discussed and agreed a new system for air liaison. Now the tragedy struck which would disable and disjoint the Chindits to such a terrible extent. Wingate took off for Lalaghat and, on the western side of the Bishenpur Hills, the Mitchell crashed in flames, burying itself deep in the earth. Everyone aboard was killed including two hitch-hiking war correspondents, Stuart Emery of the *News Chronicle*, and Stanley Wills from the *Daily Herald*.

Various possible causes for the crash have been put forward, including sabotage. Wingate was said to have ignored warnings about stormy weather. It is known that there had been trouble with one of the engines and the pilot had wanted to wait for replacement. Another theory was put forward by one of the last men to see the General alive, Jack Baldwin, later Sir Jack, who had been AOC 3 Group of Bomber Command and, briefly, stand-in C-in-C of the whole of Bomber Command. At this point, he was AOC Third Tactical Air Force RAF, formed to fight in the Burma campaign. He believed – and few men could have known more on the subject – that the pilot had shocked himself unconscious with static electricity, built up in an aerial left trailing in flight instead of being wound in, as an experienced wireless operator would have done. Switching on his set to call base at Sylhet, the pilot would have taken all the static, been knocked out and, with Wingate in the co-pilot's seat instead of the proper occupant, the result was inevitable.

The great ship Chindit, advancing into the Burmese jungle, still had engines and crew but the rudder had gone and there was no skipper who could see to the horizon. Already deployed, five brigades of Chindits would soon pass into the command of a man who had no faith in what they were doing and so would not apply Wingate's methods and strictures. Disaster and huge casualties now seemed more likely than glory which, some would be pleased to say, only proved how wrong Wingate had been.

The Japanese had columns crossing the Chindwin too, going the other way to attack Imphal, but the main story on 28 March, four days after his death, was all about Wingate. *The Times*:

'From Our Special Correspondent, lately at G.H.Q., India.

Little surprise will be felt at the announcement that Major General O. C. Wingate is commanding the Allied jungle operations deep in the rear of Japanese positions in Upper Burma. There is an unmistakeable Wingate stamp about them, above all in the emphasis that is being given to air power and wireless, the two great scientific developments of warfare; and it may now be made known that this unorthodox artillery officer had no sooner brought his expedition out of Burma last year than he was on his way to Quebec with the Prime Minister to prepare plans for a more ambitious campaign.

'General Wingate has announced from his headquarters out in the blue that his men have already established road and rail blocks 200 miles behind Japanese lines, that is, somewhere on the line from Mandalay to Myitkyina, and from the airbase so daringly established in the heart of occupied territory it will be for his columns to strike out and paralyse the enemy in his vital centres.

'His column commanders of last year now became brigadiers, the many lessons learned then were carefully acted upon, and the expedition was given a first priority in whatever equipment it requested. Now, in General Wingate's words, every man, in the midst of four Japanese divisions, is at home in the jungle, and those who marched in came 200 miles through mountains where no troops or patrols had ever been because the undergrowth was too thick and the gradients too steep.'

Wingate might have smiled at those words 'given a first priority'.

A conventional large-scale battle was developing for the Imphal plain, but on 29 March there was still news of the Chindits:

'By comparison, the Wingate operations in the heart of Upper Burma necessarily lack shape and full meaning. In the upshot they may well prove to be the more

91

Jocks in the Jungle

destructive of the opposing jungle offensives that have struck far in the rear of each other. Enemy reports bear out the assumption that General Wingate's airbase is in the region of Katha, inside the wide bend of the Irrawaddy, though from personal experience of Japanese statements about the Arakan campaign their claim to have encircled it can be largely discounted.'

Broadway, Aberdeen and the newer base, White City, were in fact on the western side of the Irrawaddy, not inside the bend, but in jungle terms 'Our Special Correspondent' was not so far out.

On 31 March the India C-in-C, General Sir Claude Auchinleck, addressed the Indian legislative assembly on the subject of the defence of Assam, and told them not to worry. He didn't mention the Chindits, or Wingate alive or dead, apart from an oblique reference to 'our forces which have been landed from the air'. On the same day that his speech was reported, the press announced that General Wingate had been killed on 24 March. Later news hinted that storms may have been the cause of the crash, and correspondents praised Wingate for proving that the Japanese could be defeated on their own terms.

Wavell wrote this soon after Wingate's death:

'He was a strange character. I cannot claim to have known him intimately, our contacts were almost wholly during the high pressure of war and on an official basis, and I do not think that he was an easy man to know. But I have no doubt about his genius as a leader, or his magnetic personality.'

In his Order of the Day to the Chindits, 2 April, Lord Mountbatten said:

92

'General Wingate was killed in his hour of triumph. The allies have lost one of the most forceful and dynamic personalities this war has produced. You have lost the finest and most inspiring leader a force could have wished for. I have lost a personal friend and faithful supporter.'

Mentions of those triumphs continued in the press for a while, detailing bridges being blown and casualties inflicted by the long-range troops, but no mention was made yet of the appointment on 30 March of his successor. Surely it would be Calvert, a great Chindit believer and a proved commander in the jungle, or General Symes, Wingate's deputy. It would probably not be his Chief Staff Officer, Brigadier Tulloch, who had no first-hand Chindit experience.

The man making the appointment was General Slim, seemingly an admirer of Wingate the man but not of his ideas. He consulted Tulloch and, with his advice, chose Brigadier Lentaigne, then OC 111 Brigade, and with that choice signalled the end of the Chindits. Slim saw Lentaigne, another ex-Gurkha officer, as a safe pair of hands (like himself). Perhaps he also saw the opportunity to put an end to all this Wingate madness.

Lentaigne, now Major General, was a fine and experienced soldier but he didn't have the ear of Churchill and he was exactly the sort to get right up the nose of Vinegar Joe, who now had the Chindits fully in his service and was their C-in-C, above Lentaigne. Wingate had seen Lentaigne as a non-believer in long-range penetration and the stronghold strategy, and so, for good reason, would never have chosen him as a successor, neither, had he been asked, would he have had him anywhere near the Chindits in the first place, much less have him command a Chindit brigade. Looking the other way, Lentaigne had seen Wingate as a charlatan; an upstart with crazy schemes. The two men had silently agreed to dislike each other intensely.

When Lentaigne took over, the Black Watch were fully in. G. G. Green's 73 Column was already on the march south towards Sittaw, near Banmauk. David Rose's 42 Column was acting as temporary garrison at Aberdeen. The Battalion's orders were to march south-west of Indaw, rendezvous at some point and block the Banmauk-Indaw road.

War Diary, 26 March, two days after Wingate's death and four days before Lentaigne assumed command: '73 *Col set off with 5 days of K rations. Marched by tracks through Manthon, crossed the Mesa river at the ford at Tanakyain.*'

Bill Lark: 'Aberdeen was no place of excitement. It was a forest clearing like any forest clearing, so we got our gear together and moved off early in the morning, single file, nobody allowed to talk. We marched all day to six o'clock. We were going to come to this chaung (pron. 'chong', a river or, depending on time of year, a river bed), and when we got there it was dry. So we headed for the next chaung, which was dry, and the next. So we stopped and formed a circle, with the mules in the centre, and we put guards out and went to sleep. First day in the new job.'

Another day of marching followed, with an alarm. Reconnaissance indicated the possibility of a Japanese ambush while, unknown to the Jocks, spotters in a nearby Gurkha column had come to the same conclusion. A Black Watch section faced a Gurkha unit, unseeing across a jungle track. Matters were resolved before bloodshed, with each side saying how lucky the other had been, that it had not come to blows.

Meanwhile, there was bloodshed aplenty at Indaw. One of Wingate's last orders had been to Fergusson and 16 Brigade.

After establishing Aberdeen, they were to attack and take Indaw immediately. Exhausted and much depleted after their long march from Ledo, they found the Japanese ready for them and in great strength.

Colonel Officer's report: *'Several days of arduous manoeuvring and sustained fire fights proved futile. The 16th withdrew toward its stronghold, in which it tried vainly to rest portions of its columns, turn and turn-about, while patrolling and skirmishing along the road leading north.'*

They had been the first in. Soon they would be the first out.

War Diary: *'73 Col arrived at Lethi, 17.00 hours. March 27, 42 Col – recce platoon and wireless sent out over Manman hills, (saw) threat to Aberdeen from Jap movements. Column dug in.*
'March 28, (Aberdeen) airstrip attacked by 7 enemy aircraft, strafed and bombed. A number of casualties included 2 of Col killed and 2 wounded. Bulldozers quickly filled in bomb craters. 73 Col hot on the march today with some paddy to cross. It was later discovered that 73 Col had been observed by Japs in Lethi village. Uneventful day however, and night bivouac was made near the main track one mile north of Settaw, 16.00 hours.'

The routine had been established during training. Standard procedure was to march in single file for fifty minutes, rest for ten. Men changed positions in their sections, sections in their platoons, platoons in their company, so that nobody was at the front – or the back – continuously. Men took turns to carry the Bren gun in addition to their packs.

'*March 29, 42 Col stood to at 05.00 and moved off at 08.15 on the track of 73 Col. Halted for the night at 18.30.*'

They left two Nigerian columns to defend Aberdeen, while 73 Col recced the village of Settaw.

War Diary: '*The Burmese guide wouldn't go in (to Settaw village) so two patrols were sent forward and contacted enemy in village. Our casualties, one man wounded; enemy casualties unknown. The fighting group occupied the village and the remainder of the Col crossed the Banmauk-Indaw road halting in a copse south of the village. The MO Capt Chesney carried out an emergency operation on the wounded man, who was able to continue on a pony.*'

This description of Chesney's work hardly does him justice. It was a nasty stomach wound requiring a complicated and difficult operation which should have been done in a fully-equipped and staffed hospital. With no possibility of that, the MO had to perform emergency surgery in the open, for a good half an hour. After continuing on his pony the man had the dubious delight of recovering sufficiently to march as before.

On 30 March new orders were received. Cutting the Mansi-Pinbon road was now the objective, requiring a change of direction from south to north-west.

War Diary: '*42 Column moved out of night harbour at 06.30 after usual stand-to, preceded by section of recce platoon having a look at 06.00 at village of Lethi. Breakfast near Nantawnauk, lunch at 12.30 to 16.30, this long midday halt being the procedure because of the heat, and to allow the wireless to be put into operation.*

The advanced recce section estimated they had seen 40 enemy armed with rifles moving east in extended order from the village of Khopyin. Made close harbour at 17.50, one mile to the east of Khopyin and sent out an ambush party on the track, in the charge of Lt Richmond.'

Further forward, 73 Column on the way to the Mansi-Pinbon road was encountering steep hills and hard going.

War Diary: *'Bivouac by 15.00. Balance of the day spent washing clothes etc.'*

While they were thus employed, an English stray wandered in. He was a private from the Queen's Royal Regiment, part of 16 Brigade which had marched all the way from Ledo to Indaw. The man had been lost for almost a week, brought to safety by a sympathetic local, and he provided the Jocks with a preview of what a long time in Burma could do to you.

Despite the fitness-inducing rigours of training, the midday heat was a severe problem. Men soon discovered that the anti-mosquito cream had the effect of blocking pores and stopping perspiration. They preferred to drip with sweat than to bake inside their own skins, so mosquito cream was abandoned.

Medical report: **'At the commencement of operations, oil of citronella in a greasy base was issued to the Force as an antimosquito cream. The discomfort produced by this obsolete repellent, and the manner in which it failed to repel culicines (gnats and mosquitos), resulted in its falling into disrepute. Consequently little faith was placed in its non-greasy counterpart when its supply became possible, and no organised parades were held to ensure its proper and regular use. Greater trust was**

placed in Dimethyl phthallate and this liquid was generally used in a more conscientious fashion. Unfortunately,
supplies of this chemical were limited and could not be
supplied in the necessary quantities.'

Later in the day, still 30 March, more new orders arrived
by wireless: 'Do not go to Mansi-Pinbon road. Go back to the
Banmauk-Indaw road and cut and block it at milestone 20.'

David Rose: 'When Wingate was killed, we were rather in
limbo for a while. Mostly we just marched, and did our officers' business on the radio with India in the evening, with
Bishop my adjutant. We only had the K rations, no fresh food,
and we didn't live off the jungle because there was nothing to
live off. It wasn't that kind of jungle where I was. It was open
teak forest.'

Bill Lark: 'A soldier lives from day to day. You do what you
do, and take everything as it comes. The best place to march
was by a chaung. You had your ordinary army water bottle
and you also had a chuggle, like a tarpaulin hot-water bottle,
and the material swelled up when wet so it didn't leak, and
you got your water from tributaries if you could, not from the
main stream. And below there the mules drank, and below
that the men washed. You had to put a tablet in the water, to
purify it. Although it was running clear you couldn't trust it.'

Bill Lark was more conscientious than some, apparently.

Extract from medical report: 'Every man was in possession of an individual water-sterilising outfit at the
commencement of operations, but as the majority of
these were of Indian-make the tablets therein had deli-
quesced. Demands were soon received on the majority
of QQs for replacements. 16 Indian Depot Medical
Stores however could not supply anything like the
number of replacements required, and those they did

98

supply were of exceedingly poor quality and really unserviceable.

'The attention given to water sterilisation was indifferent and various factors contributed to this. Not the least important of these was the lack of faith resulting from the use of the Indian-manufactured water-sterilising tablets, which on analysis proved to have little, or no, free chlorine. Again troops arriving at a water point with empty water bottles after a long and strenuous march were not prepared to wait half an hour for the water sterilising tablets to take effect, nor would the operational situation always allow of this. Moreover, the proper siting of water-points in regard to bathing was not always observed.

'A plentiful supply of English water sterilising tablets was not always available, and rather than send in nothing at all, resort was made to the use of water sterilising powder. As this was packed in 7-pound tins, it proved itself worse than useless, first because of the difficulty in carriage and secondly because constant opening and contact with the air reduced the available free chlorine content.'

War Diary: 'March 31, 42 Column headed out towards Khopyin at 06.45, turned south and proceeded over a hill path which was steep and slippery in parts. The mule loads had to be manhandled up 600 yards of bad track. Reached the watershed at 10.00. Explosions were heard from the valley. Lunch was partaken of while awaiting the return of 13 Platoon. The ambush party had been left on the track with the additional job of leading in the fighting platoon. 13 Platoon returned stating that they had encountered the enemy at Letyet and had been fired on with grenade dischargers inaccurately. Enemy received five casualties at least; 13 Platoon nil. 42 Col broke harbour at 16.00 after booby-trapping the track. Night harbour was reached at 18.30 one mile east of the village of Kanpawlut where there were many signs of recent Jap occupation – cook houses, hill slope cleared of trees. Several thousand Japs had been billeted in the area and had departed two weeks before to the north west.'

The first supply drop was due for 73 Column, which had been in for five days.

War Diary: *'73 Col still found it hard going on the hilly tracks today, and at points the mules had to be unloaded and loads manhandled. Once again an early bivouac was made at 16.00 hours. First SD two hours late because of the heavy rain, one plane failed to find the dropping area; remaining planes dropped across the flare path (rather than along it) consequently the majority of the para-chutes dropped in the jungle. One plane for 111 Brig dropped on us by mistake. Villagers very helpfully provided dry wood.'*

There were several columns in the area. A supply pilot spot-ting any sign of troops below was likely to believe that they were his designated target, he in his high-speed machine having no idea of the difference a few miles on the ground could make.

Fred Patterson: 'We were in columns but there were occa-sions when we would go off on platoon operations. It might be a week before we met up again. We wouldn't know what the others had been doing in our absence. Our war wasn't like the war in Europe; every section, platoon and column had its own war.'

Lentaigne, now in charge, surveyed the situation. His own

brigade, the 111th, had ended up on both sides of the Irrawaddy and was in the process of consolidating and heading for the Pinlebu-Pinbon road, which they were to cut, it being a main artery of communications for the Japanese. The enemy was not using air and wireless comms to anything like the British extent and so relied heavily on road and rail.

The Black Watch were marching to their new objective; the rest of 14 Brigade was to get south of Indaw and set up blocks there, also guard the approaches to White City stronghold. Other units had had various successes, blowing bridges and blocking railways and roads, cutting off Japanese supplies, and 16 Brigade was making its weary way back to Aberdeen. Nearer home, the 14th Indian Army was trying to deal with a 100,000-strong Japanese invasion heading for Imphal. In the view of many at GHQ, the Chindit brigades would have been better employed in that fight than blowing up railways.

War Diary: *'April 1, 73 Col spent the day distributing rations and cutting down parachutes caught in the trees. April 2, 73 Col had a very tiring journey today. Marched towards (village of) Le-u by track. April 3, 73 Col established road block at milestone 19 on the Banmauk-Indaw road. 42 Col had SD. April 5, 5 Pl of 73 Col moved out to milestone 17½ to cover SD which was to take place that night.'*

The supply drop began around 21.00 and all seemed in order.

Jim McNeilly: 'We'd set out on the road to assist Fergie at Indaw. That's where we were going, in our column (73), to hit the Japs at Indaw. But we'd to change and come back, and that's when our platoon went to the supply drop. My section had the flamethrower.'

This machine, officially the 'No. 2 Portable Flamethrower',

was known as the 'lifebuoy' because that was the shape of the fuel tank. It was deeply mistrusted by the men. It was indeed portable, weighing about the same as the packs they were carrying, but unreliable in use, and there was a pumping and squirting procedure to go through before it could be operated. Also, having four gallons of petrol on your back gave you very few close friends under fire.

Jim McNeilly: 'Nobody wanted to carry it. I was the NCO so I didn't carry it. For one thing, it made you a target. If the Japs saw you with it, they'd go for you right away. But that night we used it, the once, and it was once only. They were lethal weapons but for all they did, it was really not worth it, and we dumped the flamethrower after that and used the fuel for cooking.

'We'd had a tip-off that a small convoy was coming our way, so G. G. Green sent us to set up an ambush, to catch them in the valley. We waited, and three trucks came along, all full of Japs. We blew the first one up with grenades. The second one couldn't move so we took out as many Japs as we could but they fought before they disappeared, and then we had the truck for ourselves, which we used for a few days on the road until we moved off again. The third one reversed right out of it, high speed backwards in the dark round quite a sharp bend.'

War Diary: *'The supply drop was not interrupted.'*

True, but there were casualties – two killed, two wounded – although the Japanese had many more.

War Diary: *'April 6, day spent in issuing rations, burying the dead and treating the wounded. Recce sent towards Indaw. No trace of the enemy found. 42 Col joined road block. April 7, captured Jap truck used to transport 73*

Col's wounded to a landing strip for evacuation.'

David Rose: 'We used to clear a strip for the American planes called L5, which was a light aircraft that could take a couple of wounded away from pretty well anywhere.'

The aircraft was the Stinson Sentinel L5, which needed 375ft to take off, and much the same to land, at less than 50mph, although pilots complained about the brakes. Made of steel tubing covered in fabric, it could take a lot of punishment and was easily fixed in the field. The ambulance version in fact could take only one stretcher case; a second wounded man could go in the co-pilot's/observer's seat, behind the pilot, if the plane was flown solo. According to an American report, the L5's predecessor, the L1, was also used.

'It was not known at the commencement (of Chindit operations in 1944) how evacuation was to be achieved. It was hoped that light planes would be available for use in conveying casualties from the vicinity of columns to already existing airbases. Failing this, the only method possible was for casualties to be carried with the columns when they would of necessity have to be left to the care of friendly villagers, or with sufficient food and water until they became well enough to proceed on their way alone and able to look after themselves.

'With the change in plan of operations, it was soon seen that evacuation by air would be possible, and in actual fact it became so and remained the sole method of evacuation throughout the whole pre-monsoon period. Wherever possible, columns constructed light plane strips in the vicinity in which they were operating and casualties were evacuated by light plane to the nearest Dakota strip.

'These light planes were of two types, L-1 and L-5. The

former could carry four casualties (two lying and two sitting or one lying and three sitting). The L-5 on the other hand could evacuate only one sitting patient. Moreover, as the length of strip required by the L-5 was greater than that required by the L-1, the former was rarely used.'

This report does not match experience on the ground, as recalled by the Black Watch at any rate, nor the aircraft manufacturer's specifications. Also, it is known that only 125 of the L1 were converted for ambulance use in the entire war, including a dozen float-plane variants, whereas a great many more of the L5 were used for this purpose. The report is also wrong to state that the L1 needed less landing ground than the L5 and that the L5's patient was sitting. He could be, but he could also be on a stretcher, loaded through a specially fitted door at the back of the aircraft.

The 'L' stood for liaison, the term replacing 'O' for observation. The L-1 was originally designated O-49, and was the military version of the civilian Stinson Model 74 designed in the 1930s. It was really an in-between type, the USAAF having used heavier and larger observation aircraft before changing to the lighter 'grasshopper' types represented by the L5 and the Piper Cub (known as L4).

Pilots liked the L5 in the jungle because it could provide a very rapid rate of descent, which made it perfectly suited for getting into short fields, some of them pretty rough – or 'unimproved forward airstrips' as they were technically known. It was nicknamed the 'Flying Jeep' for its versatility.

The American report continues:

'Dakota strips were for the most part situated in the strongholds and were being used nightly by incoming supply planes of (USAAF) Troop Carrier Command bringing supplies and equipment into the strongholds.

These were available for the evacuation of casualties on the return trip.

'This, then, was the method used, and proved highly successful right up to the onset of the monsoon. No fighter opposition was ever experienced and evacuation was carried out continuously and without interruption.

'The conveying of casualties from columns to light plane strips was usually carried out with the help of the local inhabitants or by personnel of the columns acting as stretcher bearers. They were invariably escorted by an armed guard.'

Whether fighter opposition was experienced or not, in these unarmed little aeroplanes there was always the risk of meeting hostiles, and there cannot be admiration enough for the American pilots who worked on demand, often in appalling weather.

Many miles away from the wounded and their air-ambulance drivers, the generals were setting forth the destiny of the Chindits. Instructions from Stilwell dated 4 and 10 April, and from Slim dated 12 April, state that the LRPGs' first responsibility was to support Stilwell's advance on Mogaung and Myitkyina. General Slim designated Indaw as the most southerly point for LRPG operations, which were to be dedicated to disrupting those Jap lines of communication leading to Stilwell's objectives. Second, the LRPGs were to assist the 14th Army by disrupting enemy communications east of the Chindwin River.

Black Watch War Diary: '*April 8, Easter morning, both Columns held a church service and a communion. 42 Col had a successful SD. Soft skins (non-combat troops such as the muleteers, RAF personnel and so on) went to safe harbour where they will stay during projected attack on*

*the Jap dumps of arms at Singan. April 9, 73 Col blew
up and burned several wooden bridges near the road
block. 73 Col then moved to safe harbour near 42 Col.
April 10, SD taken, four planes, three good, one poor.'*

These aircraft were from the new RAF squadron based at
Arcan, operating for the first time with Special Force.

*'Fighting groups of 42 and 73 Cols moved to milestone
25 preparatory to attack Japanese dumps at Singan. At
10.30 hrs Mitchells bombed the area and the fighting
groups attacked the dumps. Singan was occupied at
15.00 hours. 42 Col commander Major Rose DSO was
wounded in this action.'*

Major Rose and two of his officers had recced the place the
previous day. It was to be their first use of close air support,
directing fighter and bomber aircraft by wireless from the
ground. Wingate and the Americans had been evangelical
promoters of this technique. Some of the old buffers at GHQ
were not convinced, believing that aircrew could not be accu-
rate enough to avoid hitting their own men.

On their way in to Singan, the Black Watch bumped a Jap
patrol, or rather, a Jap patrol bumped them as they were
having a breather at the time. All the enemy soldiers ran off
back to the dump, so surprise was lost and the operation had
to be brought forward. The Americans responded brilliantly.
Mitchell bombers blew the place up, Mustang fighters strafed
and, when the Jocks walked in, the Japs had withdrawn away
from the exploding munitions. Rose sent out patrols to find
them and went with one himself.

David Rose: 'We were walking through the jungle in
extended order, expecting opposition in open forest, when
we, and me in particular, came under fire. We looked in the

undergrowth to see where it was coming from, when I suddenly realised it was coming from above. The Japs had climbed up into the trees and tied themselves in. I took cover behind a tree as I was shot through the water bottle, and another bullet ricocheted off my rifle, and as I dodged the other way I was shot through my right side, in the ribs.

'My men put up a fusillade and saw to the Japs, who were not specialist snipers, just troops, tied up there. That was their tactic, the first time we'd seen it. They would know we were coming and set out to surprise, which they certainly achieved. That they had no means of escape didn't seem to bother them. If we shot them they were still a menace, because we couldn't know if they were dead.'

Jim McNeilly: 'We were as good as them by that time. We were up to and past their training, but they were there to die. The highest honour was to die for the Emperor. It was the seventh stage of heavenly grace or something. So they'd dig themselves into a hole and they'd get two or three of us before we knew they were there. Or they'd be up a tree, tied in, and rather die than give in to us.

'It was hard to fight against them. As I said we were a match to them, in some things. I don't really know how to describe them. Just fanatics. Fanatics, at all costs. We knew what we should do, but we didn't tie ourselves to a tree and expect to be shot in the tree. We weren't as daft as that. We'd save our own lives and save our own lads' lives but them, well, they were fanatics.'

Here is an extract from a Japanese report on a defeat suffered at the hands of the Americans in New Guinea. It illustrates McNeilly's point:

'It has been very much regretted that wounded men have been left behind. In the future we will give further attention to arrangements for rescuing the wounded.

However, if the wounded cannot be rescued, they must be ready to commit suicide at the proper time – that is, after all means to continue the fight have been exhausted.

'In case the wounded are retiring to the rear, always let them carry their small arms and equipment. Their ammunition should be left with comrades at the front. It is regrettable that there have been numerous instances of wounded men abandoning their weapons on the battle-field. Also, there have been instances of men leaving the front line without permission immediately after suffering wounds. This is prohibited.'

Black Watch War Diary: *'After the successful raid on Singan, large amounts of papers and documents were found, also ammunition, weapons and food.'*

The contemporary opinion of the Japanese as an entirely different kind of human being extended to views on their diet. Here is an American memorandum issued mid-war:

'Japanese Army rations have been found to be entirely edible, and ordinarily may be utilized by U.S. forces as supplementary rations when captured. If at all possible, such rations should be examined by a medical officer before being used.

'Observers (including high-ranking combat officers) recommend that U.S. troop leaders be informed about the more common Japanese foods before going into battle, so that our troops may utilize captured enemy rations if they are needed. Under other conditions, an enterprising mess sergeant may often break the monotony of his unit's diet, and add to it an unusual touch, by employing some of the less common Japanese foods. He can also use the ever-present rice as a staple

when it is captured in quantity.'

Black Watch War Diary: *'Fifteen Jap dead at the dump. The remainder of the garrison made their escape through the jungle. Casualties three killed, two wounded. Major Rose was operated on by Capt Longwell and the bullet removed from his side. Both fighting groups returned to harbour at 17.30hrs leaving the Commando pl to demolish the bridge over the Mesa river.'*

During the night, David Rose awoke feeling on top form after his operation, and decided to take a walk around the sentries in his bare feet and underwear.

'They asked after my wound, of course, and I told them I was fine, just fine, ready for anything. As I walked on I heard one Jock mutter "The Major's rather drunk" or, shall we say, words to that effect. I realised I was on a morphine high and went back to bed.'

War Diary: *'April 12, day of make and mend, 13th, day of rest. In the late morning a 42 Col patrol brought in a Burmese and an Indian who were believed to be working for the Japs. Good local supplies in this area, rice, chickens, potatoes and tomatoes, sufficient for two days, bought by 73 Col for two parachutes.*

'April 15, SD this morning was intended for the Beds and Herts. The drop was widespread and the pick-up difficult. Burman villagers assisted in the collection of scattered packages. A church service was held today.

'One patrol under Capt Swannell departed to endeavour to locate several Burman traitors in one of the small villages near Singan. The information was obtained from one Mohnsaw, a Burman from the Banmauk area who had turned from Jap informer to

ours on our arrival. The wanted men were believed to be implicated in the killing of a British officer in the Khopyin area some weeks before. They were tried by Major Condon, the Burrif officer, and were found guilty of this charge and others including dacoity (robbery with violence committed by a gang), and were sentenced to be shot at 18.00 hours. They were led away and despatched by a Sten gun firing party. Lt Austin was evacuated with a hernia. Cpl Brannen and Pte O'Brien were also evacuated – report on compassionate grounds. The Indian arrested was taken away and evacuated; the Burman was released. The SD for 42 Col at 03.00 failed to materialise and a signal was despatched for another attempt the following night.'

More bridges were blown up. Supply drops sometimes went right; sometimes went wrong. The Jocks marched almost every day, always on the lookout for possibilities of raids and damage to be done. Lots of contact with the locals kept them informed of enemy movements. This was the routine. Major Rose was on a pony, his bullet removed. All was bearable for soldiers, all except not having any definite objective with clear orders about how to reach it.

War Diary: *'April 16, 73 Col still combing the area for parachute containers while 42 Col had a successful drop. A party of villagers arrived at the harbour with presents of food for them. Another villager arrived with one of the mules which had strayed.*

'April 18, a patrol of 73 Col brought in four Burman villagers. One was the headman of the village Thitladaw, accused of sending information to the enemy. The headman possessed a great deal of Jap money.'

In fact, it came out that the villagers were on the British side. They had been sending messages to notify the Japs at Indaw of movements by British troops, which accounted for the money, but it was entirely false information volunteered by the villagers. Next day, the Burmans were sent about their friendly business.

The Japanese had flooded Burma with paper money, rupee notes, but the local people didn't want paper. Paper is no good in the jungle. It gets eaten by bugs, or dissolves in the rain, or rots away. If your small wealth was in paper, it could disappear, so the locals liked the rupee coins.

Bill Lark: 'Every man had ten rupee coins, which were like half-crowns, and when a man was hurt he could use these to buy some safety and care. In such a case we generally all gave the man an extra rupee of our own. And then we sent the Burrifs into the village. They would take their army gear off and sling a dhoti round their middles and go into the villages to get information for us. And they would say, there's a man up the track, look after him, hide him from the Japs. He's got some money and when we come back we'll give you more money, and real money, not this paper rubbish. And there would be a silk parachute as well, for the women to make dresses. The Japs dealt in paper and rape. We dealt in silk and coinage.'

The other Black Watch contingent, with the Cams, were having much the same kind of experiences – bad terrain to cross, very hard work, and occasional action.

Fred Patterson (after a day hacking a way up and over a bamboo covered hill): 'Back at road level, we split up, each platoon with a different task, blowing up a bridge or scouting a place for an ambush. I was walking down the road at night with our platoon commander Lieutenant Simpson, when he stopped me with his arm across my chest. "Don't move," he said. "There's a wire tight across my neck." We ducked under and never did find out if it was a Japanese booby-trap or one of ours.'

The ambush they set up on 19 April was a complete surprise to the Japs who were singing while marching along. It soon developed into a fierce firefight:

'Lieutenant Simpson was killed. He went down to the road for some reason and a wounded Jap shot him in the stomach. To say our platoon was shattered is an understatement.'

Patterson's much respected officer had been promoted a few days before. Captain Alexander Simpson, 24, was from Edinburgh but was actually Yorks and Lancs, seconded to the Cameronians for the Chindit campaign.

Black Watch War Diary: '*April 20, 73 Col left harbour at 06.00 following the Mesa river by track for one hour then deviated south-east through the valley of the Boncha-ung chaung. Reached the river Mesa again at Manpha. Lunch then fast march in the afternoon. Major Fanshawe went to try and find a crossing place. A recce party of 42 Col was encountered today at Thitladaw. Pte Baine missing from bivouacs.*

'*April 21, 42 Col moved to Peinnebin. Moved off at 04.00 as a stiff climb over the hills lay ahead of them. The march was uneventful and rather pleasant amongst the hills in the cool of the early morning.*

'*April 21, information received re 73 Col's projected route to the effect that water was scarce. This combined with the necessity of crossing the Mesa river, railway and then the Banmauk-Indaw road in a short interval of time meant a somewhat difficult and arduous day today. Therefore reveille was called at 02.00 hours and after some difficulty in forming up on the track, due to the intense darkness, the Col moved off at 03.30 carrying full chuggles, every second one to be used for watering the mules. Slow going in the darkness and dawn broke as the Col was approaching the river bank. A quarter of a mile beyond the river a Jap supply train could be heard. The river crossing was accomplished in the early morning light covered by the support weapons. Col reformed and moved across the road at about 07.00 and one mile past the road crossing the Col halted for breakfast, one cup of water being allowed each man. The Col moved again and marched on a compass bearing due south across the country. As a result of a recce water was found in Manthe chaung; bivouac was made here therefore at 17.00. At this harbour a signal was received that no Cols were to cross the Mesa river.'*

Bill Lark: 'We didn't know where we were going. Nobody told us. We broke camp every morning, marched all day, and camped again. When we were told to stop, we stopped. When we were told to move on, we moved on. All I knew was that we were passing trees. Miles and miles and miles of trees, we passed.

'We were to live off the stuff we carried, and when we ran out there'd be another supply drop. For a man to survive and work, K rations weren't enough in the long term. They didn't fill you when you were using so much of yourself on a jungle march. They were all right if you got some other food, something fresh, but if that was all you had then you would eventually turn into a skeleton, as we all did after months in the jungle.'

Medical report: **'Another cause of diarrhoeas (as well as bad water, poor sanitation etc.) although of more mild type, was prolonged use of the K ration. After consuming this ration for a week or two, stools became loose, watery and light yellow in colour. Fortunately, only on**

very few occasions did it prove incapacitating and generally cleared up with adequate doses of chalk and opium.'

Bill Lark: 'When it came to calls of nature we were not
allowed to leave anything on the top. We had a small digging
tool, and we used a leaf for wiping our behinds. There was
one leaf you had to be very wary of. It looked a very attrac-
tive leaf for the purpose, large and thin with a nice, soft, hairy
surface. This was another thing you found out for yourself.
Nobody who had found out would ever tell you, but if you
used this particular leaf you got a very hot bottom for the rest
of the day. Being taken short on the march wasn't really an
option, but if it was desperate you had to say "There's a Jap
in the column," and be careful which leaf you picked.'

'Using so much of yourself' on the march equated roughly
to 5,000 calories a day output, about twice what a young man
of average height and weight might use in normal activities.
Without special high-calorie foods, most men would find it
quite difficult to get that amount inside them.

Jim McNeilly was not so critical as Bill Lark: 'They were
good, the K rations, but better if you could get something else
as well. My section had been with the Gurkhas so there was
more knowledge about that. We got bananas, and there was
a tree root they called boombay, which you cut up and boiled
and it was just like a tattie. It was as good as a tattie. You
could eat bamboo shoots as well, although we didn't.'

McNeilly's boombay was not really a tree root, but the
energy-storage tubers of a climbing vine, the wild yam, sometimes called Chinese yam, which grows wild in wet tropical
regions but is also cultivated. It was probably either
Dioscorea bulbifera, called the 'air potato' for its fruits but
which has tubers like small potatoes, or *D. pentaphylla*, the
five-leaf yam. Both offered food high in starch to the
knowledgeable natives of those parts.

114

Let the US Army Quartermaster Foundation have the final word on the subject of K rations.

'Although the accumulation of research and experience has since produced amplifications of this definition, the original concept stated by The Quartermaster General in 1940 covered the major characteristics of the C ration (predecessor of K). In a letter to Maj. W. R. McReynolds, 10 June 1940, Quartermaster General E. B. Gregory stated:

There are certain fundamental principles that must be met by a ration of this type:

a. It should contain not less than 4,000 calories and preferably contain 4,500 as it has been found that this much food is required for the average soldier under field conditions.

b. It must be divisible into at least two, and preferably three, meals.

c. It must be as light as possible and still contain the necessary food value and bulk.

d. It must be suitable for use over a period of three or four days or longer, and therefore must be as palatable as possible, well balanced and not highly seasoned.

e. It must be suitable for production in large numbers and at a reasonable cost. This statement of objectives provides the guiding clue in the development of the C ration. The ration went through many changes since its formal inception as Field Ration C but basically its progression continued to be guided by the original concept of a full and satisfying ration for one man for one day and one that he could carry on his person.

'Like other unpopular items, misuse was a contributing factor to the waning popularity of the K

115

ration. Although designed to be used for a period of two or three days only, the ration occasionally subsisted troops for weeks on end. There were times when this application was unavoidable; there were also occasions when the K was employed because it was easiest to issue. Continued use reduced the acceptability and diminished the value of the ration.'

War Diary: *'April 22, stand-to for 73 Col, Manthe chaung, 05.00. Each section sent out parties to collect bamboo shoots as the mules were short of fodder.'*

Bill Lark: 'At night we fed the mules, and we used to cut young bamboo and pile it as high as we could reach or throw, like building a bonfire, and in the morning when we came out it had disappeared. We carried a certain amount of feed, and a great deal of rock salt, but the mules' main diet was what we chopped down. We also had oxen with us. We put a load on them, a fairly light load, and occasionally we'd kill one of them, and everybody got a bit of meat off it. The officers had the steak of course and we were eating the scraggy bits, but we all got some.'

War Diary: *'April 22, 42 Col moved again at 02.30 after four hours rest, marching south-east by track. The railway was crossed by the level crossing a little south of the bridge at 04.30 but between rail and road, about 300 yards along, was an enemy machine-gun post which opened fire. The leading patrol had walked through unmolested. They turned and attacked the enemy post while the path was cleared by the recce patrol. Engaged enemy firing positions in bamboo thickets for time sufficient to withdraw the mules. The Col withdrew across the railway leaving rear guard under command of Lt*

116

Richmond. Lt Anderson and his patrol were left as ambush on the track and to cover Richmond's patrol retiring. The Col reformed and marched back to the safe harbour which was reached by 08.00. During the encounter, casualties were two killed and one wounded. Enemy casualties not known but the local villagers said the Japs buried nine men the following day.

'April 23, 42 Col left Peinnebin harbour 06.00 and crossed the railway and the road without opposition, following route taken by 73 Col. Reached night harbour by 20.15 a mile into the jungle from the road. Fires were allowed from 20.30 to 21.30.

'April 24, 42 Col picked up Pte Baine of 73. He had been fed and helped by the villagers, robbed also. 73 Col moved from Manthe chaung to brigade harbour at Gahe and thence northwards to bivouac at Sedan chaung, 6 miles south of Indaw. 42 Col also moved to Gahe.'

Without an intimate knowledge of Burmese geography, it cannot be easy for readers (or writers) to appreciate what all this movement was about. With no hard information on their goals, the situation was the same for the Jocks. The two columns were marching hither and thither, as the weather got hotter and hotter, often finding themselves at the same place they had passed only days before. The Jocks may not have known where they were bound but they knew where they'd been. Remarks were made about marching up one's own fundament. More politely, G. G. Green was heard to say, 'This ought to confuse the Jap. We don't even know where we're going ourselves.'

Jim McNeilly: 'We'd patrol, criss-crossing and criss-crossing. The Japs never knew just where we were, and we never knew where they were. We didn't take them on unless we had to.'

Soundless secrecy was essential. No trace could be left to help the enemy. Cigarette ends had to be destroyed and the dust spread about, and spent matches had to be pressed vertically into the ground so they didn't show.

Bill Lark: 'If we turned off the track a certain way, there'd be a party at the end of the column who would make false footprints going the other way and would clear all signs of our passing. We never knew if there were Japs following us or not, so we had to assume that they were.

'The column was like a caterpillar, bunching up then stretching out, and if you lost your man in front you had to shout in a whisper, and if there was a problem the word would go, "Close up, there's a Jap in the column." Now, one jungle and another jungle are very similar. Indian jungles to train in, Burmese jungles to fight in. No difference. Except in Burma I heard this songbird, like I imagined a nightingale, a Burmese nightingale, and the most beautiful sound I ever heard. And one time when we all thought the Japs were charging through, it turned out to be a wild boar.'

Jim McNeilly: 'The platoons took it in turns to lead. It was a slow business, this single file. If it was your turn to be in the middle it was tedious and you slogged on half asleep. At the back you might be booby trapping, grenades with wires, and sometimes you'd hear voices, which was the Japs following us. At the front of the column you were as alert as could be, fanning out, looking for danger when you knew that, if it was there, you wouldn't see it until it was too late.'

Bill Lark: 'We stopped at this little clearing, a glade, so quiet, and the first thing as always was to take the load off the mule. Your mule was number one and you came after it in the order of things. They were very uncomplaining, the mules, they just got on with it, but you had to see they got the best possible service. I had a lad to give me a hand this time, and the back of my head bumped against something, and suddenly there was a great swarm of hornets which went for Katie. She was half unloaded and liable to run in a circle, which she did, kicking and bucking, while my pal and I ran after her being stung on the neck. I looked back and saw this thing hanging in a tree, Hornet City hanging in the air in the quietest bit of jungle in Burma, and thought the hornets would kill us before the Japs did.'

War Diary: '*April 25, Lt Nicoll returned from recce undertaken on previous day, having discovered two tracks leading to Indaw from Sedan chaung. 42 Col moved to Sedan chaung.*

'*April 26, 42 Col left Sedan chaung 06.00 on receipt of change of orders. On arrival back at Gahe they discovered that Major Fraser had left on the previous day for the Sedan chaung. Major Fraser and Coy arrived back. Reported by villagers that 4 Japs seen at Gahe observing a pick-up in the SD area. No trace of them was found. Both Cols now at Gahe.*

'*April 27, 73 Col moved out in the afternoon, followed by 42 Col, northwards to the Mesa river again.*'

Chapter Six

The Beginning of the End

By 26 April Lentaigne, the Chindit Commander in Chief, had decided that 16 Brigade was to be pulled out. He wrote a letter to the men, ready for when the airlift took place:

'You have come from the middle of Burma, where you have done your job in a manner which has thrilled the whole world you have hit the Japs where it hurts most – in the guts. (Note: this latter was a phrase borrowed from Wingate.)

'You have shown determination and endurance. You have out-manpowered and fought the enemy. You have every right to be proud of yourself.

'Now you are tired and need your rest and bucking up. I am doing my best to see you get the rest which is your due.

'Your Chinthe Badge will attract attention and comment. You must see that the reputation you and your pals have earned in battle does not suffer from your behaviour out of battle. The badge of the Force should show you are not only Special in fighting but also Special in discipline and behaviour. This is a young show which has already made a name. See to it that you do not let it down.

'There will be questions by others about your job and

experiences but there are certain subjects about which you must not talk. If you do, you will endanger the lives of those still in Burma and those who go in next time.

'*You must not tell anyone what units are part of Special Force; you must not talk about the details of how you went in or out of Burma, how you got your rations, how the air helped you, how your wireless messages were sent and received. You must not talk about your special training, equipment and arms.*

'*The safety of your comrades in Special Force depends on your loyalty and good sense. I know that I can depend on you to be discreet. Finally, you must remember that the fine work you have done is not the end of the war. We have won this round. On to the final round, and go in for the knockout.*

'*You are fully trained and know your stuff. Your job is to train the new fellows and lead them next time. Teach them to kill with every round. Teach them the jungle is nothing like as bad as it is cracked up to be. Teach them that though it is a tough job it is a man's job, a job worth doing, and one that's got to be done if you want to get back to Civvy street quickly.*

'*Good luck and I hope you have a good leave.* 26 APR 1944. MAJ-GEN COMD SPECIAL FORCE.'

The first attacks made by 16 Brigade on Indaw had failed, partially due to the poor state of the Chindit troops, partially to a piece of bad luck. Columns of 111 Brigade, passing nearby but not knowing where 16 Brigade was, or what it was doing, had tried to confuse the Japs by telling local informers that they were heading for Indaw, to attack it from the north. They were doing no such thing, but when Fergusson and 16 Brigade did indeed attack from the north, there were the Japs, fully informed.

121

A month later, another attack was more successful. On 27 April 16 Brigade, back at Indaw and reinforced with elements of 14 Brigade, achieved one objective, to take the airfield. There was disappointment even in that triumph, when it was found that the supposed all-weather strip was just another piece of grass, useless in the monsoon. In any case, Wingate's idea of a garrison at Indaw had long been dropped by Slim, and Lentaigne had already decided to bring 16 Brigade out. It looked bad to Chindit believers. Just over a month since his death, it seemed that all Wingate's crusading work had been thrown aside.

Admittedly, Fergusson and his men desperately needed rest, but they had won through in the end. Now the prize they had marched, fought and died for, was being abandoned as if nobody had wanted it in the first place.

With the additional wisdom generated by hindsight and a safe distance, it was easy for analysts such as the chief MO, Colonel Officer, to come to judgements. The withdrawal of 16 Brigade was the first act in the dismantling of the Chindits and it was seen as representative of everything that was wrong with the very idea.

Colonel Officer:

'Statistically considered, Special Force met a more dangerous enemy in disease than in the Japanese Army. Clinically analysed, it was more severely injured by malaria and dysentery than by bullets and grenades. Tactically appraised, its battle worthiness was determined by its medical discipline more than by its courage.

'During the first 45 days of the campaign, little evidence appeared that health factors would affect combat manoeuvres. Then the plight of the 16th Brigade offered an ominous but little heeded warning. The major cause of its inability to capture Indaw probably was its

122

exhaustion after the long and difficult march from India. But the inconsequence of its subsequent actions and its wholesale evacuation back to India were due to rapidly rising rates of disease and disability.

'The loss of the 16th Brigade apparently produced some regrets but no surprise or change in plans for Special Force. It had always been assumed that long range penetration groups would be used up.'

The ominous warning was the medical one which would apply to all the Chindits. Apart from the fights at Indaw, 16 Brigade had not had a major battle. There had been no big losses in the field. They had not been anywhere they might have been infected by scrub typhus, a dreadful disease transmitted by mites called chiggers, similar in biology to our own harvest mites. They live in heavy, wet scrubland where a marching or camping soldier could easily pick up the larval stage of the insect, which would feed on his skin causing a rash and itching to start with. There was no vaccine. Antibiotics were not yet available. As full blown typhus developed, the soldier was incapacitated at the least, and would very likely die if not evacuated to hospital.

Other units, including the Black Watch columns, would encounter this entirely unlooked for health hazard. Apart from not experiencing scrub typhus, 16 Brigade had not had to live through the monsoon like the others would, when living conditions that were already bad became nigh intolerable. Even so, the incidences of malaria and dysentery were so high that they alone, regardless of wounds and other illness, were enough to justify evacuation of the entire brigade.

Malaria and dysentery, as all staff officers knew, were controllable, if not preventable, by medical measures enforced through military discipline. 'Therefore,' said Colonel Officer, 'it might have been asked whether its (16

Brigade's) high sick rates could be sufficiently explained by exhaustion. This factor, it might have been thought, would lower the resistance of the brigade to all kinds of diseases.'

The implication was that the Black Watch commanding officer, Brigadier Fergusson, had allowed discipline to get slack. Let us remember the earlier words of David Rose:

'My friend Bernard Fergusson had been on the first Chindit operation and he told me what to expect. The most important thing of all was to prevent disease, particularly malaria. Fever and marching cannot go together. We had a pill to take every day, and any man who didn't take it was in effect condemning himself.'

Perhaps a different implication might have been made, had the Colonel Officer been on the march from Ledo rather than studying statistics at a desk. A Chindit might have said that weeks and weeks in the jungle, behind the lines of the most ruthless enemy, living on inadequate rations and pushing the human frame beyond the limits it was designed to take, might result in an entirely different kind of exhaustion from the one the good doctor knew about.

Morale was a serious problem and not only because of the poor diet, the inconsistent air-dropped supplies, the invisible and deadly Japanese, the heat, the dysentery and the malaria. There was also an increasing sense of it not being worthwhile. Every soldier knew it when he marched this way for days, then that way, then another way, and somehow ended up where he started. What were they doing?

Colonel Green, like his colleague David Rose, knew that discipline, including self-discipline, was the key to survival in these horrendous conditions, and one aspect of that was Green's insistence that all Black Watch soldiers would shave. Other Chindit regiments encouraged beard growing but the Jocks, Cameronians and Black Watch, were not permitted.

Fred Patterson: 'We were called the ghost force. No beards.'

Bill Lark: 'We were not allowed to grow beards like some of the other regiments, because our colonel wouldn't have it. "You're not coming out looking like those English lads (of the 1943 expedition)," he said, "wizened old men with beards. No, no, it's bad for morale." Everybody had to be as smart as possible. We all ended up looking like wizened old men, of course, but we were clean shaven wizened old men.

'I shaved with a cut-throat razor because that was what my father used. All the other boys, apart from two that I knew, had Gillettes' safety razors, and of course kept the blades. The way to put an edge on them was to strop them inside your mug, running them round the enamel mug side, or a glass jar if you were in camp. I always had my proper leather strop and I ended up shaving some of the others, who took their lives in their hands because I wasn't entirely practised at shaving anybody but myself.'

By the beginning of May, 16 Brigade was out and Aberdeen stronghold was closed down. Broadway and White City would soon follow. The Cameronians had been given orders to move north towards a defended Dakota airstrip on the Mesa River, there to draw breath for a few days, take stock, evacuate their sick and prepare for their next operation – the long march to Blackpool.

Black Watch War Diary: *'April 28, both Cols crossed Mesa river. April 29, two Cols marching together. April 30, crossed the Banmauk-Indaw road and the Mesa chaung, SD at night (early am May 1). A container with unopened parachute hit and killed a Royal Engineer attached to 73 Col. 73 Col moved on to bivvy south of the village of Alegyun.'*

This 'friendly bomb' accident was not unique. Several men were killed this way. Some supply drops, called free drops, came without parachutes, and the standard ones often had 'chutes that didn't work. The men knew all about this and sheltered under trees or any cover they could find, while the pilots above them tried to place their life-sustaining supplies exactly on the point given.

> War Diary: '*May 1, light plane landed in unprepared paddy. Day spent distributing rations. A certain number of jungle hammocks were dropped. These were of American type with mosquito net and waterproof roof. Initially they were only issued to senior officers and to the sick. They were a great novelty.*
>
> '*May 2, 73 Col marched north east to Brigade RV at Paungpila. 73 Col now have travelled approx 150 miles since leaving Aberdeen, 42 Col slightly less.*'

On 30 April there had been a conference between Vinegar Joe Stilwell, General Slim and General Lentaigne. Developing the strategy outlined earlier, which devoted the Chindits to support Stilwell, the details were set forth.

The strongholds were to be abandoned. All Chindit columns were to move north as fast as possible, to become part of Stilwell's assault on northern Burma. Mogaung was the target, and 111 Brigade was to begin by establishing a mighty block on the railway south of that town. When 77 and 14 Brigades reached the block, they would provide whatever additional resources 111 Brigade might need by then, and get ready to take Mogaung. The 3rd West African Brigade was to be deployed according to the requirements of the moment.

All of these brigades were roughly a quarter down on their starting strength, but no account seemed to be taken of that fact. Every confidence was expressed. With the possible exception of 77 Brigade, which had been in the longest, the Chindits were to operate for Stilwell through the monsoon summer.

Fred Patterson: 'By now we were tired, having been on the move for weeks. Air supply was becoming more difficult and five days' rations had to last ten days. The Brigadier (actually Lt. Colonel Masters; they didn't make him up) was pushed to move us to a very vulnerable position on a hill, which fulfilled requirements in that it overlooked the railway and the main road and had plentiful water.'

The vulnerable position became known as Blackpool.

Black Watch War Diary: '*May 3, new orders received. Btln to cross the Mawlu paddy and operate in the Napin area and to stop further Jap reinforcements from the south and SE reaching the forces investing the Henu block near White City held by 77 Brigade. The Btln was also to cover the impending evacuation of this block.*'

The Japanese had been laying siege to White City for weeks, but every attack had been repulsed in some furious fighting. Now, to the amazement of the Japs and the puzzlement of the defenders, it was to be given up.

War Diary: '*16.00 hours, a fighting group composed from both columns marched down, travelling as lightly as possible. Blankets and groundsheets were left with the combined rear elements under the command of Major Watson-Gandy. After a comfortable march in the cool of the evening on a path leading due north, both Cols halted for the night at 19.15.*'

Jim McNeilly: 'Our job was to keep the Japs from getting to the front at White City, but we were not to engage them, just get information. There was no action, just patrols. We came across them, but we didn't attack. At the end of one day, we were on one side of a river and they were moving on the other side. We didn't fire a shot. They probably knew we were there and didn't fire a shot either. We were stalking them and they were stalking us. If we went off-track, the last platoon booby-trapped it. Grenades with trip wires.'

War Diary: '*May 4, a march for a mile up the chaung helped to hide our tracks. A mule convoy of 17 mules under the command of Lt Noble returned to the old area to collect the various articles of small kit left behind by the battle group. Continuing the march north, contact was made with a patrol from White City. Progress was now very difficult as a trail had to be cut, up and down the ridges (of the Kachin Hills), in very hot weather. Information was received that a Jap patrol was occupying the village of Napin.*'

A Burrif recce group investigated Napin and found no Japs because a West African column had cleared it two days before and was in possession. The villagers of Napin preferred Chindit occupation to Japanese and helped with a supply drop.

War Diary: '*May 5, strong ambush party of three patrols under command of Major Fanshawe* with one 3 inch mortar in support moved off to the track which the enemy was believed to be using at night. 15.20 – a force of seven enemy planes flew low over the harbour on their way to strafe and bomb White City.*' (**John Fanshawe was an officer of the Argylls who had volunteered for Chindit duty.*)

Bill Lark: 'To the ambush we took three mules, two with radios and mine with the hand grenades. I had the hand grenades then because Thrushie Joe, which was Menzies' mule, couldn't take them as he was sick. Grenades are very dangerous in the jungle. You throw one and it's liable to hit the branch of a tree and come back.'

The route took them across a plain of elephant grass, following the locals' animal tracks, and over the railway. The fighting men carried only their weapons and ammunition, grenades, water and rations. It took some hours longer than planned.

Bill Lark: 'We got there and were put in our places, about twenty yards behind the ambush line, and we thought it's going to be another of those useless exercises when we should be asleep. We'll be up here all night and nothing'll happen. It was eleven o'clock, bright moonlight, and we were all lined up along one side of the road.'

Normal practice would have been to mine the other side, to cause mayhem among Japanese fleeing from the ambush, but there hadn't been time.

Jim McNeilly: 'There were two platoons who laid the ambush, and our platoon was one of them. Our sergeant was Sgt Blair. I think it was Sgt Ballantyne on the other platoon. Some of our boys had been in Tobruk and Crete, but the rest had never seen any action like this. So we had to cool them down, tell them to keep quiet and let the Japs through us into the trap. We didn't know exactly what we were going to, how many Japs. We were just told a fair amount of Japs. And up they came, up the brae and, would you believe it, an officer on a great white horse, and all these men behind, slugging along with their heads down.'

Bill Lark: 'When they were well in, the signal was to be firing the last Bren gun, but when they fired it, it went "plop", and again "plop", so they changed the gas port, and "plop", so they shouted "bang" or something, and all hell let loose.'

Jim McNeilly: 'Someone took out the officer, I think it was Geordie Ballantyne, and then it went mad, just mad. The Japs were screaming, their mules were screaming – theirs had voices, ours didn't – they were braying and kicking. What a noise, rifles, and Brens on spray.'

Bill Lark: 'The officer was shot off his horse by Private McLuskie. The horse went galloping up the road, then everything happened. When we opened up, what a racket. They all seemed to have high-pitched voices, and they were screaming and shouting. We always used to say, the answer to noise is silence. We never made any noise. In the jungle they used to call, "Come on Tommy, where are you, Tommy?" We were firing down the ranks and lots of them fell. In the dark, when you're fired on, you have no idea what it might turn out to be and so you run, and they did, skedaddled away from the road. I was standing by my mule, Sten gun at the ready, when I heard men crashing through the trees. It was dark. I was going to fire, but it was our lads on the move. Then it happened again. Talk about nervous wreck.'

Jim McNeilly: 'There was no fear of them attacking us. If they had we'd have been finished. They'd have over-run us. The story was there were over a thousand. And then it was over and we withdrew. Each and every man looked after each other, so we withdrew and got all together again. And the commanders decided to do another one the next day.'

Bill Lark: 'Next morning there were dead Japs lying on the road and they'd all had their right hand cut off to send back to the relatives to cremate. We lost three dead and a dozen wounded, including a Dundee lad, Boozy Broon, who we made a bamboo stretcher for. He was in a very bad way and died later.'

This was Corporal Murdoch Brown, age 33. His body was moved after the war from the battlefield cemetery at Sahmaw to lie at Taukkyan War Cemetery.

Bill Lark: 'Our burial party brought back bags of rice and bits of dried fish that we said was shark's fin but I don't suppose it was, and we threw it away anyway. And bags of iced gems, those little round biscuits with an icing star on, hard icing, except the biscuits were like dog biscuits and the icing stars had all come off and were mixed up in the bag, so we threw away the dog biscuits and ate the icing. So that was their rations, the Japs, rice, dried fish and dog biscuits. It's a hard life being a soldier in the jungle. We were grateful for the rice. It made a great change from K rations.'

Here is another American report on Japanese army rations, which confirms Bill Lark's view of them:

'Contrary to the belief of some persons, the Japanese soldier does not live entirely on rice. To him, rice is a staple food, just as bread is to us; and, if he had only rice for his meal, he would be as displeased as we would be with only bread to eat. However, rice does constitute well over 50 per cent of the Japanese soldier's diet.

'Both polished and unpolished rice have been captured from the enemy. Polished rice is more common, probably because it can be preserved longer than unpolished rice. To increase the palatability of rice, the Japanese usually season it with a soy-bean sauce (shoyu) or miso paste, which is made of fermented soy beans and which is more commonly used for preparing soup.

'U.S. rations weigh more and have a higher calorific value than the Japanese.

'Although the Japanese have standard rations, they supplement these whenever possible with various foods obtained locally – even when standard rations are easily available. Two types of specially packed field rations, "A" and "B", have been noted frequently. The "A" ration normally consists of 30.7 ounces of rice, 5.3 ounces of meat or fish, and a small amount of seasoning and flavoring. The "B" ration normally consists of 24.4

131

ounces of hard biscuits in three paper bags (enough for three meals), 2.1 ounces of meat or fish, and a small amount of seasoning (salt and sugar).

'Emergency air-crew rations found recently in a wrecked Japanese plane (New Guinea) included 20 ounces of unpolished rice and the following other items: puffed wheat, biscuits, a dried fish, two small bottles of concentrated wine (35 per cent alcohol), some candy wrapped in colored cellophane, large salt tablets, and a portable water-purifying set. These items were divided among five transparent, water-proof bags.

'Probably the most common type of Japanese canned food is compressed fish (principally salmon and bonito), which may sometimes require soaking and salting to make it palatable. Other items of Japanese food found included: pickled plums, dehydrated vegetables (beans, peas, cabbage, horseradish, burdock, seaweed), compressed barley cakes, rice cakes, canned oranges and tangerines, sake (rice beer), powdered tea leaves, slices of ginger, salted plum cake, canned beef, cooked whale meat, confections, and vitamin tablets.

'The Japanese soldier has a fondness for sweets, which he usually gets in "comfort bags" sent from home. He also is issued sweets at certain times, along with a ration of sake. Such issues are usually made to coincide with a Japanese national festival or holiday.'

War Diary: '*May 6, Major Fanshawe and the ambush party returned at 07.45 and reported that at least 100 enemy had been ambushed, 14 bodies were counted, one of them the officer who had led the column on a white charger. Own casualties were three killed and three wounded, one of whom died later. (Other reports give more wounded, possibly fourteen; all were flown out next day by light aircraft.)*

   'May 7, both Cols moved off together and reached night harbour at 15.30 hours. In the early evening, 6 Pls under Lt. Col. Green left to lay ambush on track north of Nathkokyin. Remainder of Bn under Major Rose stood by to assist main ambush party.'

The ambush was supposed to be a diversionary tactic to keep the Japs occupied while Calvert evacuated White City. It turned into the biggest single action the Jocks had seen so far in Burma. The six platoons numbered about 200 men.

David Rose: 'I was in charge of the soft skins, and the fighting units would flee to me when they withdrew from the ambush. I was the rallying point organiser.'

The ambushers waited and waited. It was the same track as had provided the action before, but a much bigger fighting party hoped to inflict rather more damage. It seemed that the Japanese were not going to oblige and so, at 04.55, G. G. Green ordered his men to fall in on the track and head off south, back towards Rose and safe harbour. They progressed for twenty minutes, until the platoon at the front of the line saw a group of the enemy 'sitting and moving about the track', as the War Diary put it, about fifty yards away. Some accounts have suggested that the Japanese were unaware of any danger and that an orderly and disciplined attack ensued. Eye-witness reports and the War Diary make it clear that the Jocks saw, and were seen.

War Diary: *'Both parties cleared the track simultaneously. On orders, two platoons were to advance down the left of the track and two down the right. 5 Pl cleared the ridge by bayonet on the right of the track. Firing broke out all round.'*

Jim McNeilly: 'We weren't at the front this time. They liked to give men a break from that, to try and get our minds together. Well, it didn't work too well in this case because at first it was chaos. The sergeants tried to keep their platoons together, or gather them together more like it.'

War Diary: *'Japs counter attacked and took ridge from 5 Pl. Further advances made south along track and the battle seemed to be going very much in our favour except for a small pocket of Japs on the right which repeated efforts had failed to dislodge. Enemy formed up two counter attacks which were both beaten back by our fire before they could be pressed home. The CO then ordered the party to move down the wadi (or chaung, possibly) towards Nathkokyin and took up position on the crest of a hill near the village.'*

Back at the safe harbour, Rose and his soft skins listened to the battle.

War Diary: *'From 05.25 hrs until 10.30 hrs machine gun and mortar fire heard continuously. At 10.35 hrs Lt Anderson reached harbour area with his platoon (which) had been separated from main ambush party but had broken through the enemy by a bayonet charge.'*

Anderson brought no information on the whereabouts or well-being of G. G. Green and the majority of the ambushers. David Rose was scheduled to move his harbour back to Napin no later than 16.00. There was time yet for all to end well, but news was needed. He sent out patrols, including Burrifs, who were to try and gather intelligence on Jap movements. Major Fraser came back with some, but not all, of his men, and news of the fight but not of the CO.

At around 10.30am the noise of battle had ceased but no one at the harbour could tell what that meant. All three results were possible – victory to one side or the other, or stalemate. At 11.30 came a kind of answer when the firing began again. Fraser went back out again with a fresh patrol and the Burrifs came back.

War Diary: '*100 enemy reported in the village of Nyaungbintha with approx another 500 south of it. A message was sent to White City for 25 pounders to shell the village. Firing (at the battle) had continued spasmodically until 13.30 hrs. Shelling commenced at 13.35 hrs.*'

Enemy forces around Green's position at Nathkokyin had been estimated at 200, and there would be more nearby. Green was down to 105 men and eleven wounded. Four o'clock came and, knowing that Rose would be on the move, Green ordered dispersal.

Jim McNeilly: 'It had been supposed to be an ambush but we met the Japs head on, and in the morning they got up to fight and they got all around us. We fought them but we couldn't hold for ever, and the bugle blew dispersal. Platoons stuck together but it was every platoon and every section to fight for itself and to find a way back to the rendezvous. There were three rendezvous points at different times, but if you didn't get there you were on your own. They wouldn't wait for you. It was down to the NCOs in the sections to navigate and map reading in the jungle is no easy matter. You had to make decisions. My eight men, my lance corporal and me made my section, but none of the others could read a map. This bit of a track looks exactly the same as that bit, but you have to decide which one to go down. We only had three days' rations with us and, with not going back after the ambush, we were a day late as it was. After that, I always had my section carry an extra day's worth, if we could get it. There was a lot of wounded. G. G. Green had most of them with him.'

War Diary: '*(The remnants of the ambush party) moved north along the side of the hill range and bivouaced for the night in the hills. At this time the Col was without food but luckily had full water bottles.*'

War Diary: '*By roll call (at the harbour) it was found that 150 men were still missing with the CO. Reports came in that the enemy were digging in, and burying their dead.*'

They had a large number of dead, too, and wounded. Fraser came back at midnight to say so. He'd seen them.

On the morning of 9 May the harbour party made an airstrip, anticipating an airlift for the wounded they had there and the others they expected would arrive. The L5s were busy, but no news of Green.

War Diary: '*May 9, at 14.45 hrs the ambush party arrived back to the remainder of the Battalion in an exhausted condition and were eagerly welcomed by their comrades. Mess tins of tea were brought to the boil and the wounded treated at the RAP. A happy reunion indeed. The CO and party had been cutting their way through difficult and mountainous country all day since breaking harbour at 06.00. Two men had died on the way and another had had to be left behind owing to a smashed femur. He was left near a village whose few remaining inhabitants were told they would be well rewarded if they cared for him. One man (Pte McGregor) had walked for two days blind and Lt Richmond had hobbled along shot through both feet. Information was received that Lt McGuigan and Lt Nicoll had been killed. A thanksgiving service was given by the padre, near the RAP so the wounded could join in. The turn-out consisted of every man who was able to leave his duties.'*

David McGuigan, 24, was from Ayr. Douglas Nicoll, 23, was from Broughty Ferry and was shot by a sniper while speaking to his Colonel, wearing a white bandage over a head wound.

Of the eleven wounded Green had begun with, there were only eight to load onto the aircraft.

Jim McNeilly: 'The L5s came in, the Yankees, onto that little airstrip. They were great, just great.'

Losses were calculated as best they could. It looked like twenty-six known killed, thirty-five wounded, some, not many, unaccounted for. Against that were Jap losses almost certainly heavier, and the successful evacuation of White City.

War Diary: *'A congratulatory letter was received from Gen. Lentaigne on the important role played by the Black Watch.'*

Chapter Seven

Monsoon

The monsoon in Burma was supposed to break on or around 25 May, and plans had been laid accordingly. The rains started on 5 May, not too seriously at first, but building up quickly. By 15 May, no weather forecast was necessary. The monsoon was upon them, with inches of rain falling almost every day.

Jim McNeilly: 'Next day (10 May) we were on a forced march right away, a non-stopper, across the valley through elephant grass. You couldn't see anything. You just hoped that the leaders had picked the right track. They called it the 'Valley of Death'. It became a swamp in the monsoon. We had to move pretty quick because we were very short on rations and there was a lot of elephant grass to cross. The platoon sergeants had walkie-talkies, otherwise we'd have had no idea where anyone else was. We were away to the brigade safe area, where there was going to be a big supply drop, with another five days' rations and ammunition.'

The forced march was part of the plans for the Jocks and the other Chindits laid down by Stilwell, Slim and Lentaigne at the end of April. Wingate had never meant his LRPGs to stay in the jungle for long after the monsoon begun, and he would not have stood for it, Vinegar Joe or no. The new plans seemed oblivious to the seasons, to the evacuation of 16

Brigade and the reasons for it, and the depradations already being suffered by all the other columns.

Jim McNeilly: 'After the rains began, you just couldn't ever get dry. I never wore socks in the wet, which was a trick I'd learned from the Gurkhas. They never wore socks, and had boots one size smaller, and they never got blisters like we did, so I tried it. I had just a bandage round my heel and my instep and wore a size seven instead of an eight. Some of my section did the same. It worked. No blisters. Which was one less thing to worry about.'

War Diary: '*May 11, the village of Konkha reached and a quantity of (Japanese) army rations found. The village was duly fired.*

'*May 14, Btln moved to Nami chaung. Preparations made for supply drop. Major Rose was by this time having trouble with the bullet wound he received at Singan. The wound had broken open again with skin trouble around the wound.*

'*May 15, SD at 02.00 very scattered and only two and a half days' rations could be collected. The bulk of the Btln's Sten guns dumped awaiting disposal by light plane. These weapons have been displaced by carbines, a more dependable weapon for rough usage. Heavy rains commenced; monsoon looks like breaking. Handed over four mules to West Africans before leaving. 73 Col broke harbour at 15.00 for the start of the arduous march over the Kachin Hills. Night biv reached on a chaung at 18.00 hours after a slow march over a slippery, muddy hill track. May 16, 42 Col moved out, the start being delayed by heavy rain.*'

Stories went about that the Africans were short of mules because, not liking the K rations at all, they'd eaten their beasts of burden and the four replacements would go the same way. No firm evidence has been found for this allegation.

Over the next few days the rain became so heavy that marching was almost impossible. The Kachin Hills, on a scale similar to the middle ranges of the Scottish Highlands but cut by steep, almost vertical valleys and covered in tropical rain-forest, made for difficult terrain in any weather.

David Rose: 'We would have been fine if hadn't been for the wet. We'd been told we wouldn't be left in during the monsoon, but with Wingate's demise, that was forgotten. We weren't prepared for a long endurance campaign. We didn't even know when the monsoon was due to start, and it came quite suddenly.'

Jim McNeilly: 'That was when my extra day's rations came in. That day we were caught in the monsoon, a lot of them had no meat, but we had meat. The others asked where we got the rations. We said we carried the damned things. They were all right, the K rations. They gave you enough for marching and what you were doing, but not enough to keep disease away. That was the killer, the diseases we had when we were weak.'

Bill Lark: 'Ah, good Lord above, the monsoon. We had one special wool blanket which was thin and light, and an army groundsheet. You'd put the groundsheet down and lie on that, wet, with the blanket on top of you and let the rain fall. Or you'd wrap yourself in the blanket and then the ground-sheet and huddle under a tree and try and get some sleep that way. But the rain did act like a shower bath. It washed your clothes and you at the same time.

'And the leeches; the leeches that dropped on you. They got in some funny places. How they got through your clothes and in between your toes I don't know, but they did. And every-where else. The boys used to touch them with their cigarette ends and they curled up and dropped off. I didn't smoke but we had mosquito stuff too, and a wee dab of that did the very same thing. They were about three quarters of an inch long, and they must have been able to sense you in some way, because they dropped off the trees onto you and you never felt them. You'd never know you had them until you took your boots and stockings off and saw them there, between your toes, sucking your blood.'

Modern readers must remember that non-smokers were the exception in those days, and among soldiers even more so. Cigarettes were very important.

Bill Lark: 'When we were in training, in India, the lads used to chuck their cigarette ration because they were so awful. They called them "spitfires", because that's what they were, and because there was a picture of an aeroplane on the front of the little packet that had three cigs in. They would make their own arrangements to get hold of tins of Player's or what-ever. So, I collected the spitfires. I guessed they would come in handy one day. So off the boys went on a four-day route march, without the mules, and I stayed behind. I would be going with the truck they sent out with the food, and would take my bag of fags that nobody wanted. I said, "How are you getting on, lads?" and they said, "Just fine but we could do with a smoke." I said, "I've got the very thing." They said "thank you" and smoked the lot. When you've got nothing, anything will do.

'One day in Burma, one of our lads, he was from a gypsy family, was cleaning his gun, a Sten gun, and he hadn't checked for ammunition; if it was loaded. There was a bang and a bullet shot past me, and an officer appeared from nowhere and saw me. "Who shot that?" he asked. "You stupid so-and-so. You could hear that for miles." Well, it obviously wasn't me as I didn't have a gun in my hand, so the officer put two and two together and pointed to the gypsy lad.

"Put him on a charge," he said to me. In the middle of the jungle, I ask you, put him on a charge. So he came up before the Colonel, G. G. Green, next morning. I went through the usual spiel, adding that the silly sod could have killed me, and the colonel said "Three days CB," which is confined to barracks. We didn't exactly have any barracks, so that was changed to three days with no cigarettes. "You," the Colonel said to me, "make sure that when he opens his K rations, he gives you the cigarettes." I did, but I knew what those cigarettes meant to the men who did smoke, which was just about all of them, so I gave him them back. I said, "When you fancy a draw, get yourself out of everybody's way. And if anybody sees you, you didn't get them from me."'

Jim McNeilly: 'We heard that in other columns they used corporal punishment for stuff like insubordination. So many lashes with parachute cord. But not in our lot. You got a talking to, or ignored in certain cases, but for worse things there was a sort of solitary confinement. Say, some lad let off five rounds at nothing because he was jumpy. The officer would give him one day in the jungle on his own. If he got back, that was that. I used to say, if you get lost, find a river and follow it against the flow. Keep going upstream, and you'll end up in China.'

War Diary: 'May 19, 73 Col *reaching end of a very tiring hill march over muddy and slippery tracks arrived at Brigade RV at Mainthengyi, and bivouaced at Mainthi chaung. Very damp and depressing biv and all ranks rather exhausted after march from Konkha area. 73 Col received one day's rations from the Yorks and Lancs. 42 Col had SD. No move today – much needed rations distributed.*

'May 20, 73 Col *rested at Mainthengyi and great use was made of the chaung for washing and scrubbing muddy clothes. May 22, 42 Col reached Brigade RV at mid-day after being delayed on this hill march by bad weather. 73 Col moved out once more after having two supply drops in the last two days and harboured at Namsai chaung for the night. Heavy rain most of night. May 23, rain so serious that nothing could be done. 42 Col without rations so first bullock was killed. 73 Col had successful SD.'*

Any supply drop at all in this weather was something of a miracle. Wireless transmission/reception was often interrupted. Sometimes the weather was so foul that not even the Americans could fly in it, and if they did they had the extremely tricky task of finding their rationless troops in very poor visibility.

War Diary: *'May 24, Major Rose's wound had steadily worsened and the skin trouble around it was enlarging greatly. Having had very little sleep for the past nine days the Col commander decided he had to be evacuated here at Mainthengyi. Major Michael Condon of the 2/Burma Rifles assumed command of 42 Col.'*

Condon had been a civilian in Burma before the war and knew enough of the language and dialects to get by – a considerable asset. Some of the men thought him lacking in LRPG experience.

David Rose had refused to be evacuated but, as time passed, he realised that the right decision had gradually become the wrong one:

'I was ten days on horseback as a casualty and the wound was getting worse. I had appalling prickly heat, but so did many of us. We had dreadful casualties because of sickness. We were marching wet, resting wet, sleeping wet, and never dried out, so you got these tiny pimples, one in every pore over your entire skin.'

Definition of prickly heat: In humid conditions, an irritating skin rash caused by dead skin and bacteria blocking the pores, especially where there is friction, e.g. with wet clothes. Medical name, Miliaria. In severe cases, salt crystals form in the sweat gland ducts producing small blisters. Scratching the itch is of no benefit and can only lead to skin infections.

David Rose: 'I began to realise that I was losing my cool and was getting rather ill-tempered and that kind of thing, so I told them that with great regret I should have to give up my command. They left me and half-a-dozen West African wounded beside this little airstrip they'd built.

'A staff officer from Brigade came across us lying there and blew his top a bit. He said that the column commander must not be allowed to fall into the hands of the enemy because they'd torture him. That was me, and presumably I'd let out a few secrets. Presumably also, it was more permissible for other ranks to fall into said hands, because they wouldn't know anything and so could only be used for bayonet drill. Anyway, this chap was an old Burma hand and he'd been in the government forestry department and knew a thing or two. He rounded up some elephants, the idea being that if the L5s couldn't fly because of the monsoon, which was getting seriously underway, they'd take me by elephant to the Indawgyi Lake.

'I had no idea about any of this. I was just waiting by the airstrip with these other chaps for a lift out of it. The plane came and the first passengers were a badly wounded man in the Nigerian regiment and me, but it couldn't get off with both of us in so, unbeknown to me, he was put out, and within an hour I was in a wonderful American hospital. So when the elephants turned up, I was gone but the others were still there. They went by elephant to the lake and, a few days later, were taken off by flying boat and came to the same hospital. Some of their wounds were maggoty by then but they were all saved.'

The new man Major Condon represented the only time in that war when Black Watch Jocks answered to a permanent Commander from another regiment. Wherever he was from, the routines stayed the same. After two months in the jungle, the Jocks were still almost entirely reliant on K rations.

Bill Lark: 'We would come across hens running around and the officer would say, "Ah, we're obviously near a village." But they were wild jungle fowl, like a kind of hen to look at, a foreign, Burmese-style hen maybe, but a hen. We'd have loved to have shot them but we daren't make a sound like that.

'When the supply drop came, sometimes we'd all have a little onion each, and sometimes there was bread. Bread meant that the men at the other end, back at base, were giving up their rations for us. This bread we got looked like it had little currants, but were the bugs that lived in the flour cooked in it. Naturally nobody complained about that and we ate the lot like it was the finest fresh loaf ever baked and sliced for a man.

'The Burrifs came off best. They knew what you could pick and eat. Nobody told us you could eat bamboo shoots. After all that time in the jungle, with bamboo growing all around us, the first time I knew about bamboo shoots was when I had it from a Chinese restaurant, years after the war. One day I saw a Burrif up a tree, eating berries. He threw some down to me and they were just little brown berries, and you put them in your mouth and got the most powerful sour taste which then changed, to sweet and delicious.

'On the march, every man had to carry 100 rounds of ammunition, which went in pouches on the pack, and in another pouch you put your powdered milk sachet which you squeezed out and made last for five days. The mules had what was called numnah – I think that was the word – pads under their saddles. It was hairy stuff about half an inch thick, and we used to cut a strip off this and fit it to our pack straps as cushions, which helped a bit with the seventy pounds you were carrying. You had the ammunition, plus blanket and groundsheet, one set of clothes – socks, shirt, vest, maybe trousers – five days' K rations, two hand grenades, first-aid kit, mess tin, bayonet, bottle and chuggle. On your belt hung your Dhar, which was a Burmese type of machete, to chop your way through. And when you've got all that lot on you, you've got some weight I can tell you.'

Extract from Colonel Officer's medical report:

'The weight carried by the men was far too high. It is one of the elements of Military Hygiene that the weight carried by the man should never be more than one-third of his body weight. Anything over that reduces the man's efficiency and capacity to physical effort. That, in the case of a soldier in battle, means the reduction in his power to move, to seek out the enemy, and to success-fully engage him in combat.

'The average weight of the men in one column was 145 pounds and yet the weight carried by the Bren gun carrier amounted to 95 pounds; in other words, he was carrying about two thirds of his body weight or twice what he should carry. The lightest weight carried was 67 pounds – the weight carried by a rifleman armed with a carbine (with rations all eaten) – which is nearly half of the man's body weight. There is only one answer to this problem and that is that anything over the optimum man-load must be carried by someone or something else. It means increasing the tail but it also means increasing the fighting efficiency of the fighting soldier. In the Chinese Army every third man is a porter.'

Porters? Yes, well, we can see Wingate agreeing to that. And that 145 pounds was the average starting weight. By this time, most of the men had lost a considerable amount, but the packs stayed the same.

The plan had been for the Black Watch to reinforce 111 Brigade as needed, and then go on to attack Mogaung, but before they could reach the block – Blackpool – the situation had changed. Blackpool was not really a block, being about a mile away from the railway and road which it overlooked, and holding it was becoming more difficult as, in Stilwell's eyes, it became more imperative. If he was to succeed in the north, Jap supply lines must be cut. Where, he wanted to know, were the reinforcing columns of 77 and 14 Brigades? Lentaigne's answer was to ask for discretionary powers to abandon Blackpool, these powers to be delegated to the man on the spot, Jack Masters, in command of Lentaigne's old unit. Attempting to reach Blackpool, Lentaigne felt, could reach the point where a choice had to be made between total destruction and flimsy chances of survival.

It was not an ideal site for a stronghold in any case and many who were there believed it had been established in the wrong place. It was too easily approached and attacked.

Fred Patterson: 'The Japs were sending up troop trains that we (Cameronians) weren't allowed to interfere with. Into the middle of May they started in earnest, shelling and mortaring us. Every aircraft that came in to our strip was taking out wounded and sick. The monsoon started and our numbers were dwindling. Then we lost the airstrip and things were getting grim.'

The Cams had been in Burma for two months and sickness was taking hold. Platoon strength averaged twenty-five instead of forty-five, and there were not enough men to do everything needed – pick up supplies, set out barbed wire, dig in, patrol, form a defensive garrison, and all the rest. The Japs brought up six anti-aircraft guns which made supply drops even more difficult.

At this point the Dakota airstrip had been shelled to uselessness and 14 Brigade was still miles away. Stilwell did not like it at all. Was 111's predicament so bad? What was to be gained from leaving a stronghold, only to have to creep through a jungle full of Japanese? Were 77 and 14 Brigades trying hard enough to get to Blackpool?

In fact, by the time David Rose was evacuated, Blackpool had already fallen.

Fred Patterson: 'The rain was torrential, food was low, and ammunition almost gone when the signal came to withdraw. As I jumped out of my trench, the Japs moved into one 15ft away.'

At a conference on 25 May Lentaigne and Stilwell debated, argued, or restated their positions regarding Blackpool. Both were equally determined, with additional new points from Lentaigne about the health of his troops. Food and ammunition were short enough among the beleaguered garrison and the likelihood of sufficient supplies coming in was low indeed, but on top of that, there was no possibility of an airlift to evacuate the sick and wounded, whose numbers were rising rapidly. They would have to be carried through the jungle. Further delay might make such a job impossible.

Perhaps so, was Stilwell's opinion, but to him the block seemed essential. He wanted Mogaung and believed he could take it with his Chinese army, provided the Japanese were stopped from bringing up reinforcements and supplies. Surely that was a task ideally suited to Special Force? Wasn't that the idea? Wasn't that what Wingate had been banging on about? And if not, what was the use of Special Force?

Facing an insistent Lentaigne, Stilwell backed down and agreed to delegate discretionary powers to the commander of 111 Brigade, then learned later that Blackpool had been abandoned the day before anyway. Not unnaturally, being the limey-hater he was, Stilwell believed that Lentaigne had tricked him into giving permission after the fact.

It is hard to see what else Jack Masters could have done, other than take the responsibility. Through the night of 23 May and into 24 May, his men had suffered terrible casualties. The Japs were crawling across the airstrip. Artillery, mortars and aircraft were bombarding relentlessly. No relief could be expected from anywhere and the weather was appalling. The whole situation was hopeless.

Figures at this point for 111 Brigade were afterwards stated as 82 killed, 206 wounded, 49 missing, 318 evacuated sick. The number of those wounded carried out of Blackpool on stretchers is uncertain. Quite what was going to be done with them, should they reach any kind of safety, was likewise unclear. Stretcher-carrying in itself was an extremely difficult matter in the jungle. Theoretically, it took eight men to carry one; four to carry the stretcher, four to carry the packs of those with the stretcher, then turn about. Needless to say, theory did not often apply, and a frequently used alternative was a Gurkha-style bamboo contrivance dragged along by a mule.

One piece of good fortune arose from Japanese inflexibility. Instead of stopping the shelling and closing in on the near-helpless remnants of 111, probably wiping out large numbers, they stuck to their timed plan and unwittingly allowed the withdrawal. The Cameronians, by now amalgamated into one column only, acted as rear guard as the Brigade began a five-day march towards the Indawgyi Lake. That this would prove to be a ghastly nightmare was obvious – it was appalling weather with only one-and-a-half days' rations per man, and no wireless to call any more.

There now followed one of the most desperate and heart-churning episodes of the whole expedition. There were not enough mules and ponies to carry or drag the wounded. Men with wounds were carrying comrades who had worse damage. The Japs were not far behind and the British were in no fit state to fight. The MO reported that nineteen of the wounded would never make it. Others with a better chance needed those stretchers or they would die too. Jack Masters made the awful decision, and the nineteen, to spare them from capture alive, were shot.

Black Watch War Diary: '*May 25, 73 Col biv in the village of Nammun, a somewhat rare occurrence. 42 Col left Mainthengyi. May 26, 73 Col left Nammun and marched north in company with Brigade HQ and two Cols of the Yorks and Lancs, the expectation being a reinforcement/support task to help 111 Brigade who were holding a railway position called Blackpool against besieging Japs, eight miles SE of the top of the Kyusunlai Pass. The message came that 111 Bde had been forced out of Blackpool the previous day so the task was changed to holding the Kyusunlai Pass at all costs, to prevent the Japs using the pass to reinforce their positions at Kamaing. At 17.00 hours 73 Col's rear elements went back to Nammun while the fighting group headed for the pass. 42 Col meanwhile reached Nammun.*'

Jim McNeilly: 'We got new orders to defend a pass over the Kachin Hills called the Kyusunlai, so we had to get to the top. We were to keep the pass long enough for 111 Brigade to reach us. They'd had a terrible time trying to hold a position on the railway, Blackpool it was called, and they had masses of wounded. The rains had come by then, and we had engineers with us whose job it was to hack down bamboo and build a staircase up the mountain to get the mules up. And sometimes a mule would go over the edge and topple down with all its stuff and be lost to us.'

War Diary: *'May 27, after a wet and uncomfortable night, 73 Col battle group reached the top of the pass and took up positions on its crest. The many wounded of 111 Bde were struggling up the pass and were met at the top by 73 Col. May 28, 42 Col left Nammun for the pass, listening to the sounds of intense firing coming from it. Japs shelled the ridge all day. May 29, mule convoy of 42 Col went to Nammun for rations and on their return reported Jap snipers at water point. Japs continued their efforts to dislodge the Jocks and take the pass.'*

Bill Lark: 'In the few times it stopped raining, we could look down into the valley and see the railway. One day there was a train on it and our planes were attacking it. It was like a show at the theatre with us in the best seats. Fantastic.'

The Jocks were not only on the crest, of course. Having slogged their way inch by precipitous inch through the mud to the top of the mountain, men were sent slipping and sliding down the other side to defend against Jap attack. The reason for holding the pass would shortly change – from seeing the wounded and sick over it to preventing the Japs interfering with the evacuation from the Indawgyi Lake by flying boat. If the pass was open, the enemy could bring up artillery to shell the lake, and anti-aircraft guns to shoot down the relatively cumbersome Sunderland aircraft, of which there were only two – nicknamed 'Gert' and 'Daisy' – available. (For younger readers, Gert and Daisy were the stage names of a popular female comic double act of the time, real names Elsie and Doris Waters who, incidentally, were the sisters of Jack Warner, who later played Dixon of Dock Green.) If lakeside facilities could be built – jetties, field stations – and a 'flare path' was marked with buoys, and there were enough rafts, boats and DUKW landing craft, the Sunderlands could take away forty casualties at a time.

151

The aircraft, of 230 Squadron RAF, normally based in Ceylon (Sri Lanka), flew 537 men of 111 Brigade from the Indawgyi to the Brahmaputra River and took in supplies and reinforcements, between 2 June and 3 July.

Jim McNeilly: 'We sent a lot out in those planes, but they were only the ones who looked like they might make it, make a recovery, you understand. I don't know what happened to the others, the hopeless cases. We never saw them again.'

War Diary: '*May 30, 73 Col support platoon attacked Jap positions in the valley with mortars while another patrol engaged the enemy on the ridge to the south. In the afternoon it was 42 Col's turn to be shelled. Snipers still active at the water point.*

'*May 31, enemy shelling and mortar fire continued during the morning. Ration party of 73 Col returning at 16.30 hours was fired on by Jap snipers at water point. One man killed and two mules wounded. Commando Pl discovered Japs on the ridge to the south and engaged the enemy. 16 Pl of 42 Col attacked Jap mortar positions.*

'*General situation – food scarce, weather atrocious, under constant attack on all sides.*'

Bill Lark: 'Going to that water point on the pass with a mule was a decidedly dangerous adventure. The mule didn't know about snipers and just wanted to get to the water. The muleteer couldn't abandon his beast and couldn't really stop it either, so the Jap had two targets, one very nervous with two legs and one oblivious with four.'

The Battalion's officers had been expecting to be on the pass for a few days, but that turned into weeks. Casualties fell regularly from the shelling, but mostly happened when Jocks were out on offensive patrol down in the valley. It was marshland, elephant grass, with water sometimes up to the waist and not at all suitable ground for any kind of military action, offensive or defensive.

Very soon after the conference of 25 May, General Lentaigne began to suggest that Special Force was finished. It had lost its ability to make a significant contribution, he believed, and the best option was to conclude all its operations. The alternative was a combination of sickness and battle casualties amounting to annihilation. Stilwell wanted the Chindits to move north to support his attacks on Kamaing and Mogaung. This was no longer feasible, Lentaigne felt. His men were exhausted. It was too much to ask of them to march all that distance and then expect them to fight the Japanese. Current evidence showed that Stilwell's Chinese were not going to advance quickly enough to reduce the task, and large numbers of Japanese were in the way. Any sizeable actions by Special Force would be too costly. The only thing to do was to pull out now. The worst of the monsoon was to come, bringing with it renewed, and perhaps insuperable, difficulties in dealing with sick and wounded, especially the sick who were expected to be numerous.

Stilwell's response was to order the remainder of 111 Brigade to stay in a position to harass the enemy, but Indawgyi Lake was the priority for the moment. Whatever Stilwell wanted them to do, the Brigade's commanders put saving their ailing men first. Meanwhile, Mike Calvert reported 77 Brigade temporarily sick as a fighting unit, stating that the men were no longer capable of moving quickly for any length of time. As the monsoon shut down the possibilities of guerrilla warfare, 77 Brigade headed at its own pace towards Mogaung and a more conventional kind of battle.

Black Watch War Diary: *'June 1, Jap snipers infiltrated (again) to positions overlooking the water point. West African patrol sent out to destroy the enemy and were successful in that the Japs withdrew. Very heavy rain and oppressive atmosphere.'*

These snipers were the result of repeated attempts by the Japs to sneak in at night. They were repulsed on every occasion. The African soldiers were led with verve and vigour by Captain Douglas Ross of the Black Watch:

'June 2, 42 Col sent patrol under command of Capt Dalrymple to bottom of pass. They bumped a party of Japs on return journey. Capt Dalrymple wounded (hand) in this action and later had to be evacuated.'

There was something of a story to Hew Dalrymple's retirement from the Chindits. His was a small patrol, with his rear covered by another unit watching the track by which he was to return. There was a mix-up. The covering patrol left the track early, Japs came through, and David Rose's old friend Hew met them when expecting no opposition.

'June 3, reorganisation of perimeter force by Capt T D Ross. June 4, 42 Col sent out patrol under command of Lt. Wallace to patrol high ridge immediately above and beyond their positions. They engaged the enemy and Lt Wallace was killed. Sgt. Kennedy brought the patrol back safely.'

According to the Commonwealth War Graves Commission, Lieutenant Archibald Mitchell Wallace, of Dundee, age 25, was killed on 2 June. Archie Wallace had been in the process of occupying his new position when the Japs came in with a surprise attack. Other casualties were four wounded. A witness also places the Wallace incident before the Dalrymple wound, so we can assume the war diarist has the days transposed.

Headquarters staff of 14 Brigade were at Nammun, supposedly to take advantage of an airstrip there and co-ordinate supplies, but the airstrip was by no means monsoon-proof. On 6 June Brigadier Brodie left Nammun to take command of the Jocks on Kyunuslai, while G. G. Green led a force of 73 Column and one of 42 Column under Captain Ross, on a long patrol to investigate another mountain pass. The monsoon was going at full strength by now, and the men who had to live in the swamps around the Indawgyi Lake were falling victim to scrub typhus. This disease can take the strongest men down, and these Jocks were severely debilitated and in low spirits just from their working conditions. Everything was wet. Anything that could rot, did so. Anything that could rust, did so. They rested in stinking mud and walked all day in it. It was virtually impossible to light a fire. Whether or not there were Japs around the corner, they had to behave as if there were.

Green's patrol saw very little action but almost every man was sick with dysentery and/or malaria. Even the men who had so far resisted, and who religiously took their malaria medicine, were now falling victim.

Back at Nammun, supply drops were coming in regularly, mostly K rations but supplemented occasionally with bread and bully beef and more frequently with rum.

Jim McNeilly: 'When you rested in a safe area, you were getting respite from the Japs but not from the disease, and not from the general depression. Sometimes we would have a kirk parade, which was good for morale. Everybody went, whatever their religion, because the singing cheered you up. There we were, singing hymns in the jungle, while the typhus crept up on us. We didn't know its name at the time but we knew what it did. You were all right one minute and away the next.'

The battle for north Burma was building up to a climax. While Stilwell's Chinese headed down from the north

155

towards the Kamaing-Mogaung-Myitkyina triangle, Stilwell ordered the Chindits to harass and disrupt the enemy from the south and make their way for the final assault.

So far, 14 Brigade, the most recently in, had lost 151 men to sickness; 71 had been killed, 95 wounded, and 27 missing. From 77 Brigade, 269 men had been evacuated because of sickness, while other casualties were 172 killed, 415 wounded, 84 missing, and 11 captured. Inevitably, as the fighting grew harder, the monsoon rained more heavily and disease struck ever more virulently, the worst was yet to come. At Blackpool, it had been generally known among 111 Brigade that this was the final job and would be followed by a return to India. By 6 June, with all the sick shipped out, the last men standing were at the north end of Indawgyi Lake waiting for their order to go home. Instead, they were told they were going to support Stilwell's advance on Mogaung.

Fred Patterson: 'We had been promised a return to India and possibly home leave. Instead we were reorganised. We only had sufficient men left to make up one column (out of the original five).'

All of what little there was of 77 Brigade attacked Mogaung. To block retreating Japanese, 14 Brigade was to follow the route the enemy would take, but in the opposite direction.

All through the month of June, the various fragments of Special Force manoeuvred, marched and attacked in the worst possible circumstances. The Japanese were well dug in, their defences fully prepared and their communications well established. They knew the Chindits were there, so there was no advantage of surprise, and the previous benefits of rapid mobility – the chance to hit and run – were gone because of the weather and the poor physical state of the men.

As the fight for the Kamaing-Mogaung-Myitkyina triangle

156

went on, Special Force became weaker and weaker but stuck to its duty. On 11 June 77 Brigade reported that the attack on Mogaung had been extremely costly. On 16 June Calvert warned Stilwell that there was very little fuel left in the tank. The promised Chinese support had not arrived and, unless it did, the Brigade would have to give up. Very shortly, he'd be counting 500 men fit to fight, and that was all.

As ever, Stilwell was sceptical to say the least, largely because the casualty figures he had took no account of the physical state of the walking wounded and unwounded. The statistics said that Calvert should have had 3,000 or more on his strength, but the majority of those were in no state to battle with Japs. They were exhausted, monsoon-beaten, suffering from trench foot, sand-fly fever, malaria, jungle sores, and utter weariness. Similar messages were coming from 14 Brigade and 111 Brigade, which only served to irritate Stilwell even more.

Bill Lark: 'When the mules got a sore, it would be infected and the flies would lay their eggs and maggots hatched out. That gypsy lad, he had a sore and found maggots in it. We used to leave them until the wound was clean and then pick them out with tweezers.'

Black Watch War Diary: *'June 21, soft elements left Nammun village and halted in the foothills near the lake to await the arrival of the Battle Group from the pass. June 22, fairly hard going owing to the mud. 42 Col in front having difficulty finding correct track. June 23, very hard going owing to mud and hills.'*

These were the parts of the Kachin range directly north of Indawgyi Lake which offered the easiest passage compared to the nine and ten thousand footers to the east and west. These were only around 3,000ft to 4,000ft above sea level, 2,000ft above Jock level on the ground, like the Scottish Highlands but steeper, covered in trees, and favoured with a couple of hundred inches of rain a year. Once over, they'd be in the valley through which the railway ran, which, the assumption was, they'd be able to block.

The mud on what passed for tracks was often up to their knees, the rain was non-stop downpour, and word came to 42 Column that the village up ahead was home to 200 Japs and some elephants. A Burrif scouting patrol found that the Japs had left, so the Jocks gave themselves a twenty-four hour stopover. When the locals heard what was intended as a route, they pointed out that in their view – and they should have known – the way was impossible for man or mule. Brigadier Brodie disagreed and went on to look. The consequence was a lot of hard work.

War Diary: *'June 24, REs now building steps up the hills, the only possible way of getting over the range.'*

It wasn't just the engineers, naturally. Jim McNeilly: 'In the monsoon we had to build steps up every hill. It was a chance to rest between shifts, which you took turn and turnabout. We all chipped in. We had to build the way up, and then actually get up it with the mules. Very tiring.'

Bill Lark: 'One lad who was behind me kept saying he wasn't going to make it. So I said, "Give me your rifle and hang on to my mule's tail," and we got him along that way.'

War Diary: *'June 29, after a wait of four days, Col moved out to tackle the job of getting up the hills, four men being detailed to each mule. Track littered with all sorts of broken harness and dead mules from previous Cols which had used the track. Going hard for everyone as the steps are so high. Col bivouac in Nawku village.'*

Starting at 05.00, elements of 42 Column reached the top of the Nawku Pass at 19.30, losing four mules and a wireless set. Perhaps the villagers had been wrong about being able to get through, and the Brigadier was right.

Stilwell, meanwhile, was becoming increasingly dissatisfied with Special Force. He had won some of his arguments with Lentaigne but the pressure was mounting from the higher command, Slim and Mountbatten, for the evacuation of the whole Force. There was yet another conference on 30 June. Lentaigne said most forcefully that the Chindits must be relieved. In particular, he said that 77 and 111 Brigades were in a 'very exhausted state and their stamina so lowered that they were unable to resist disease and sickness. Only about 350 men of these two brigades are really effective.' They had done their duty. Mogaung had been taken by the remnants of 77 Brigade (26 June), which had almost obliterated itself in the process. The Chinese could see to the rest of it.

Stilwell replied that there were enough men left to do some sort of damage, with no need to keep sick men in the line. The region around Mogaung was not clear of Japs, and any that were there could be sent to reinforce the enemy garrison at Myitkyina. Further, there might be a counter-attack on Mogaung. The area had to be secured and held. We had the advantage there and we had to keep it. Special Force must remain, to do what it could.

After struggling through swollen rivers and over jungle-covered hills, the Cams and the raggle-taggle rest of 111 Brigade reached their RV, expecting to be provisioned and rested before an assault on Mogaung. That they made it there at all was partly due to three magnificent elephants and their mahouts, performing all manner of stirling duties.

Fred Patterson: 'Most days they gave us a two-hour start. They looked big and clumsy but their ground speed was amazing. One of them gave our mules a rest by carrying our wireless and generator, but an elephant loves water, which fact had been overlooked, so it lay down in a river we were crossing and that was the end of our wireless.'

It was soon the end of the elephants too, when they were shot at by someone in a light aircraft who must have imagined they were in Jap employ. This was not part of the bargain, the mahouts decided, and off they went.

Without elephants, more bad news came. The Brigade was to join with a column of Gurkhas and turn back to the south east, to clear the Japs from the Mogaung valley as the town had already fallen to 77 Brigade.

Mountbatten and Lentaigne drew one concession from Stilwell. There would be a medical survey. The sick and 'unduly weak' would be taken out, while the rest would concentrate on aiding the assault on Myitkyina, keeping Jap reinforcements and supplies out by patrols and roadblocks.

War Diary: *'July 1, a day spent in checking equipment and trying to repair and improvise girths for the mules. July 2, patrols, which were out in the direction of Pumkrawng, reported that conditions were worse than the Mokso side of the hills (which they were then climbing) and that it would be impossible to proceed at all.'*

So, the locals were right, but the Brigadier wasn't giving up just yet. Perhaps he knew of Wingate's edict: 'No patrol will report a jungle to be impenetrable, until it has penetrated it.'

On July 3, to enable 73 Col to move off, 42 Col gave them all their girths, so they (42) were now dependent on a supply drop of girths before they could move. 73 Col and Brigade HQ moved off but their progress was very slow. Arriving at point 3177 recces were sent off to the east, cutting their way through the jungle, but after a time it was found that it was

160

quite impassable for mules. There was nothing left but to retrace their steps to Nawku, bivouacking for the night at point 3177 in pouring rain. 42 Col sent a patrol to Latang where Japs had been reported digging in around the village.

The patrol, led by Lance Sergeant Todd, came under fire from the dug-in Japs, and the Burrif scouting out front was killed. Todd took his men round the flank, recced the village and attacked the Japs from behind, killing a number. Back at the bivouac, L/S Todd was made full Sergeant Todd. The War Diary describes this incident as 'a slight skirmish'.

'July 4, 73 Col returned extremely tired, covered in mud and soaked to the skin. Successful supply drop today included large quantity of gifts. Cols now mobile, where mud allows. The following plan was decided at a conference of the Brigade Commander and Column Commanders. All soft skins, under command of Major Watson-Gandy, to return with mules to Mokso and proceed to Lakhren, and thence across the hills to Pahok where the Battle Groups would join them in about three weeks' time. The Battle Groups would proceed without support weapons, wireless etc. to the area of Namkwin Chaung to join a Col of 7th Leicesters who had mules with them, and proceed to the original operational area from there.

'July 5, the rear colns and support plns of 73 and 42 Cols combined into one body and left the Battle Groups at Nawku at 06.30 hrs. Their intention was to join up with Battle Groups at the village of Pahok on the other side of the hills. The march to Mokso was completed in a day. The first signs of foot-rot began to show at this time. The Battle Groups remained in Nawku today preparing for the move tomorrow.

'July 6, 73 Col Battle Group moved off with Brigade

HQ, followed an hour and a half later by 42 Col. The route was along the first boundary track then SE to Namkwin Chaung, a distance of 16 miles. It took the Cols five days to cover this indescribable piece of country.'

Contrary to the conference, arguments in 42 Column reversed the decision not to take wireless. They regretted it in some ways, having to carry such heavy equipment through the worst conditions anyone had ever encountered, but at least they did have some contact with the world beyond the mud. Minds were changed also on the subject of mules, and some were taken to carry the expected sick and wounded, although the animals slowed progress even more.

The Cameronians were experiencing the same horrors. Marching on yet another last job, it took them five days to cover twelve miles, and they could cover no more without a rest for their feet, skinned and raw, and an attempt at recuperation for their skeletal frames. They did take a small village from the Japs, but patrols were largely futile. No movement was possible except along what might have been tracks before the monsoon, and all such were closely watched by the enemy.

On 1 July, 111 Brigade was ordered to advance, led by the Cameronians into an attack on a high point held by the Japanese. Next day, after reviewing the situation and counting about ninety non-disabled, the Cams' commanders agreed that this order could not be carried out. The only option was to report the Battalion as unfit for action.

For the next two weeks they would be placed on light duties, helping to build an airstrip near Kamaing, by laying brushwood and then metal mesh on a piece of swamp with a hill at one end and trees at the other. They also lent a hand with evacuees, before the last march that really was the last,

162

24 July, thirty miles to the nearest Dakota airstrip and out by aircraft. Fred Patterson had already gone, one of five men knocked down by malaria and crammed somehow into an L5, one of whom was discovered, as they began their take-off run, to be lying on the control wires.

As Fred said, 'How we cleared that hill only the good Lord knows.'

War Diary (with soft skins): *'July 7, more aircraft arrived but not the numbers that were required. The colns were still short of everything bar K rations. A sick convoy went off to Indawgyi Lake, mostly cases of chronic feet and typhus. July 8, quite a good drop of clothing but still short of (mule) fodder. Major C V Watson-Gandy commanding rear coln told Brigade Major 'No grain, no move' for 2nd Battalion. July 9, goods arrived. We stocked up and started for Lakhren, a village about 23 miles from Mokso and situated at the top of the Indawgyi Lake. The going was extremely difficult.'*

War Diary: *'July 10, moved at 07.00 hrs. After lunch we left the main track and turned in through the jungle but there was very little improvement. Bivouaced by a large chaung at 18.00 hrs and brewed up.'*

For the battle groups, the last part of their trek involved chaungs and gorges which, out of monsoon season, would have been a relatively easy stage. Where chaungs would have been dry, they were now rivers. One was 2ft deep and, as 42 Column waded along, the level rose another 2ft and the flow increased beyond the ability of the men to stand. They took refuge on outcrops of rock and waited an afternoon and a night for the flood to abate, with their few mules all but submerged.

War Diary: *'After very slow and extremely hard going through some of stickiest mud yet experienced, 73 Col arrived at the RV across Namkwin Chaung and met up with the 7th Leicesters. The whole area was muddy and filthy.*

'July 11, 42 Col followed the track made by 73 Col and reached the RV about mid-day. Supply drops frequent and most things issued from Brigade dump. Most people now suffering from foot-rot due to perpetual wet mud and sand from the chaungs. (with soft skins) Ponies are all being used for casualties with foot-rot. Reached bivouac area at 15.30.'

A two-day rest was ordered for the battle groups, with laundry done as best they could. Two days was nothing like enough, of course. They needed months, not days. Some of the Jocks' feet hardly resembled feet at all.

War Diary: *'July 12 (soft skins), six more miles to do today. The going got better and reached bivouac area. We are now in contact with rear Brigade by wireless. July 13, feet are worse still. Moved at 07.00 but had not gone 400 yards when we met Cameronians and Brigade was 1,100 yards away. After an hour we were all in our allotted areas.'*

Fred Patterson went in search of an old Black Watch pal, Peter Reid. 'They told me he had gone out with the recce party the previous evening and had been found with typhus and covered in leeches in the morning. He'd been taken to the hospital.'

Peter Reid, 21, from Kinlochmoidart, died on 15 August and was buried at Digboi in India.

David Rose had reached Calcutta and hospital, his prickly

heat still giving him hell, though his bullet wounds were healed. The Matron came to see him. She turned out to be one of the nurses who had looked after him while he was recovering from his Somaliland wound.

David Rose: 'She was a Scots lassie called Bremner. Quite a character, and she sorted me out right away. She had me put in a bath of dilute potassium permanganate, then I had to dry like the washing, without a towel. Matron Bremner produced a huge pot of Pond's Cold Cream, with which I had to cover myself. I had the first decent night's sleep in weeks.'

Such luxuries as a good night's sleep, available to the evacuated, were not commonplace among those who should have been out long ago. On 13 July in the early afternoon, the Jocks in the battle groups left Namkwin for Kawan. The going was heavy but not as bad as before, and 73 Col found Kawan late on the 14th while 42 Col arrived the next morning.

War Diary: *'Kawan already occupied by a coln of Yorks and Lancs. Having collected several days' rations 42 Col recce with a section of Burrifs pushed on towards Pungan while 73 Col put in a surprise attack on Lollaw Bum. This was entirely satisfactory, catching the small number of enemy on the wrong foot.'*

The soft skins expected to stay at Lakhren for three or four days but the news was that the RV with the fighting groups might be changed. They stayed for eight days, while the sick got what treatment was possible. Feet were rested, animals were fed, soldiers' rations improved and spirits rose a little. Signals came to the effect that the Black Watch could expect to be flown out of Myitkyina about the middle of August, although that airfield was held by the Japanese at the moment.

By laying bamboo mats, the Black Watch made an airstrip that could be serviceable in the rain, and the L5s were busy again taking the sick away. As the War Diary stated on 20 July:

> *'It is obvious that many will not march the next leg and will have to be evacuated by plane or sick convoy to Kamaing. We have lost about 35% of our strength including three officers. All serious cases are being flown out.'*

Flying-out policy when the columns first went in to Burma was straightforward. If you fell sick, you kept going until you became a liability. Because you had been so healthy and fit through the training before you went in, and through the hard work in the jungle before you fell sick, you were usually evacuated before the sickness could damage you long-term. This was so, even though you had kept going beyond the point where, in any other kind of warfare, you would have been admitted to a field hospital.

The policy worked well enough for the first weeks and before the monsoon, and numbers of evacuations were small in any case. After the monsoon began, the hard work and the monotonous diet in those extreme conditions began to have the reverse effect. Physical fitness deteriorated. In this weakened condition, by the time a man became a liability, permanent damage could have been done to his constitution.

Worse, the chances of evacuation had almost disappeared in early May when the Dakota airstrip at Aberdeen was lost. Apart from the short time of the flying boats at Indawgyi Lake, that left only the L5 ambulance service, much curtailed by the monsoon. When the other strongholds fell, with their light-aircraft strips, there was nothing for the L5 pilots but extempore landing grounds in mid-jungle.

166

Despite these difficulties, the evacuation rate rose from five men per thousand per fortnight in March, to 115 per thousand per fortnight by the middle of July. The men who carried on suffered three or four malaria attacks which lowered natural defences against dysentery, diarrhoea, lung infections, prickly heat, jungle sores and so on, which in turn had a greater effect than normal. Add general debility, anaemia and malnutrition, and only the few men with cast-iron constitutions could hope to come out without their long-term health jeopardised.

Chapter Eight

The Last Few

Officers out in the field often felt they had more important things to do than file reports, including the weekly medical summaries they were supposed to send in. Deprived of such information, before the survey results were in, the only way the chief HQ medic for Special Force, Colonel Officer, could be sure of the medical situation was to fly out regularly to the battle zones, the hospitals and the casualty clearing centres such as the one by the Indawgyi Lake, to see for himself. The monsoon stopped him from doing this as much as he wanted, but by mid-July he felt he had seen enough to describe the situation accurately:

'The state of health in all Brigades is very much the same and is, taken all around, extremely poor. All have lost anything from two to three stones in weight. The incidence of fever is steadily rising and there are few men who have had less than three attacks of malaria. The majority have had as many as seven attacks, and all have been treated within their columns.

'With the onset of the rains men are constantly wet, both day and night, and have little or no chance of getting dry. Paths are in many cases waist deep; and foot rot and prickly heat, which very quickly turns septic,

*have become rampant. Deaths from cerebral malaria and
typhus fever are common and on the upgrade.'*

The senior MO of 14 Brigade wrote:

*'In a week or two's time the number of deaths due to
sickness will absolutely stagger the authorities. But we
have sounded the warning, don't blame us. Soon the
sickness will be quite beyond our control. Eleven deaths
from fever at Plymouth last week.'*

Plymouth was one of the two evacuation stations on
Indawgyi Lake, below 2nd Battalion's old positions on the
Kyunuslai pass. Another MO in 14 Brigade reported:
'General health is undoubtedly deteriorating at a rapidly
increasing rate due to (1) the frequent occurrence of short
rations and (2) the continued wet weather.'

Since 14 Brigade had left the swampy valley where scrub
typhus was endemic, some improvement had occurred,
Colonel Officer reported, by which he meant only that the
rate of contracting scrub typhus had fallen. Elsewhere he
found columns 'Severely debilitated. Weight loss, anaemia
due to malaria and fatigue' had almost entirely incapacitated
most of the men in terms of ability to fight and move rapidly.
Marching five miles a day with half-hour rests every hour,
was about as much as could be asked.

The recommendation from Colonel Officer was for immediate withdrawal. Even then, the men would need at least
three months' recovery if there was to be any thought of
deploying them again in this war.

More evidence came with Lentaigne's medical survey.
According to the column medical officers, the figures being
used by Stilwell were wildly out. The strength of 14 Brigade
was down to sixty officers and 1,100 men, plus those waiting

for evacuation. Of 77 Brigade, 75 per cent were permanently or temporarily incapacitated. The temporary ones would mostly turn permanent if they were not hospitalised soon. The total in 111 Brigade was a few more than 700 officers and men listed as fit for duty, which was the minority as over 1,100 were unfit through sickness. The 3rd West African Brigade, much better off than the others, was still a third below strength.

Comments made to the survey by column medical officers were unequivocal. 'These men are near mental and physical breakdown.' 'Half of the fitter men have foot rot.' 'The fit men are at 40-60 per cent efficiency.' 'Column commander states men will not attack further unless led by outstanding officers.' 'Of the fit men, 70 per cent are weak from previous diseases.'

Sick rates were still 'rising alarmingly'. Basically, Stilwell had just over half of the officers and men he had thought he had, and almost all of those were unable to operate adequately.

Lentaigne sent an aircraft for Calvert and took him to meet Stilwell. It was Mad Mike versus Vinegar Joe. Calvert, avoiding emotional language, told Stilwell that he had entered Mogaung with the last seventy of his effective troops. There had been no more. 'After this my men were completely exhausted and flat on their backs.'

He admitted that the disposition of his much-reduced force after Mogaung had not been precisely according to the orders received from Stilwell, but that had been because they couldn't get to where the General wanted them. They simply could not do it anymore.

Stilwell realised that he had, in effect, been out-manoeuvred. 'All very polite,' was his comment afterwards.

The Supreme Allied Commander, Mountbatten, sent Stilwell some advice on 16 July. He referred his American

170

colleague to the original schedule as devised by Wingate, by which 77 and 111 Brigades would have been relieved by 1 June and 14 June, and the 3rd West African Brigades would have been relieved by 30 June.

The Supreme Commander could hardly order Stilwell to bring the men out. He had, after all, agreed on 30 June to keep them in. The most he felt he could do in the circumstances was to remind Stilwell that whatever was left of 77 and 111 should be evacuated after the fall of Myitkyina and, similarly, the remnants of the rest of the Chindits should be brought out as soon as possible after that.

As Mountbatten and Stilwell were fully aware, the siege of Myitkyina had become a stalemate and, without the full amount of hoped-for interference from the Chindits, the Japanese were bringing up reinforcements. To cap it all, Stilwell's own American and Chinese troops were beginning to suffer the same medical problems that had floored Special Force.

Lentaigne kept up his campaign to have 77 Brigade lifted out. Stilwell kept saying "no". Lentaigne changed tack slightly, asking for permission to order 77 to stop fighting, to retreat to safe harbour somewhere, and to evacuate all men who were not fit for work. To Stilwell, this seemed no different to total evacuation, so he told Lentaigne to carry out the orders he already had. Stilwell heard Calvert's reaction second hand, but remained unmoved. The commander of 77 Brigade said 'Cannot anyone realise that we are finished and fought frantically to the end before we defeated the Japs and that when we beat the Japs they remain beaten?'

Vinegar Joe was not finished yet, encouraged, Lentaigne believed, by a particularly antagonistic American staff officer who fed disinformation to Stilwell and thus fuelled his dislike of limeys. On 19 July Stilwell summoned Lentaigne to a meeting. It seemed to the American that 14 Brigade was disobeying orders, and so was 111 Brigade. What was going on? Of course, he knew what was going on. He had Lentaigne's signals in front of him.

Yesterday, Stilwell noted, Lentaigne had instructed 14 Brigade to change from its position as ordered, and move to relieve 111 which, according to information, had been directed to break off the attack Stilwell wanted, at Taungni, on the railway below Mogaung, so that it could evacuate its sick and wounded.

Lentaigne could only acknowledge that he had acted on his own initiative. On 17 July an independent medical commission had examined every man still with 111 Brigade. Four doctors – two American, two British – and six nurses concluded that all were suffering from malarial fever and amoebic dysentery, with an average weight loss of thirty-five to forty pounds.

Unlike so many other diseases, the contracting of which renders you immune for the future, amoebic dysentery, caused by a parasitic single-cell creature dwelling in watery places, makes you more susceptible to further attacks, and very unpleasant they are. To quote from a contemporary medical textbook:

'In bad cases the bowels may move one hundred times a day or more. The fever varies in amount but there is always considerable thirst, scanty flow of urine, nervous depression and great general prostration.'

Considerable thirst in those suffering from a waterborne sickness compounded the liability to more of the same, often leading to liver abscesses. The treatment nowadays is with drugs not discovered in 1944. Then, the patient was prescribed 'a large dose of powdered ipecacuanha root, preceded half an hour before by 20 drops of laudanum to lessen the tendency to vomit. The patient must be kept in bed, warm, and on a low diet; milk, beef-tea, and arrowroot, in quantities of not more than a small teacupful at a time, being the only articles allowed.'

Should the Chindit MOs find themselves a little short of ipecacuanha (a powerful laxative from Brazil), beef tea and warm beds, the usual prescription was low-diet K rations and get on with it.

The examining medical commission also found typhus, foot rot, rotten teeth, jungle sores going septic, all kinds of ulcers and bites, dengue fever, etc., and only seven officers, twenty-two BORs and ninety Gurkhas could be considered able to fight.

Lentaigne's admission to using his own initiative, according to American records produced the following dialogue.

Stilwell: 'I have never objected to getting out the sick and wounded. I do object to a change in missions.'

Lentaigne: 'I had to do it. I had to take action to safeguard my men.'

Stilwell: 'Certainly we must all look out after our own men. I intend to make a case out of this. You are not obeying orders. You have not made an effort to keep me informed.'

Lentaigne: 'You have been away a good deal of the time.'

Stilwell: 'Yes, but I do not recall any efforts to contact me.'

Lentaigne: 'I felt that I had to do it because it was desperate.'

Stilwell: 'We have tried to get to Taungni. New orders have been issued to relieve one unit making an attack, and to move in another unit that, I thought, was on another mission. I do not see why we should give up the ghost when there are 5,300 effective men.'

Lentaigne: 'The 111th Brigade is absolutely finished.'

Stilwell: 'It is agreed that the sick and wounded should be evacuated. I cannot see why you issued these orders.'

Against his better judgement, Lentaigne offered to rescind his orders, which was no new thing for the Jocks and all the others on the ground. The men had not yet reached their new positions, so it was not too late. Stilwell wanted to know if there were any Burrifs or other Kachin auxiliaries who could move swiftly to the aid of the sick and wounded and help evacuate them. According to the American staff officers, there were none. What about Chinese transport troops? They were all fully occupied already.

Stilwell: 'I understand how you feel about the sick and wounded. We all feel the same way.'

Lentaigne: 'The big question at the moment is taking care of the wounded. The remaining effectives are in very bad condition themselves. The feet are absolutely raw on some of the men. They have been wringing wet for a month or more. There is no sunshine in those jungles. Another thing we have just found is that almost every man is full of worms. This is probably because they have been on K-rations ever since they have been in. Malaria is a constant source of trouble, the men are taking from three to four Atabrine tablets every day. There are many deaths due to sickness.'

Stilwell questioned the reliability of the reports on troop numbers, perhaps thinking the British might have under-counted in some way. Not at all. Lentaigne replied that figures were fine, but that's all they were, figures. They represented only numbers of sick men, not fit men.

'On a recent visit to 111 Brigade,' he said, 'they were actually rude to me concerning their condition of sickness. Those men are carrying 70lb on their back. They are nothing but skin and bones, plus all the other forms of sickness.'

Stilwell's response was that all units must hold their positions until he ordered otherwise, but the sick and wounded 'will be withdrawn'.

Lentaigne would not give in. The MOs in 111 Brigade were quite clear and would say that there were no men fit to fight. In which case, Stilwell wanted know, how was it that the latest statistics he had, showed that there were more unfit men in 14 Brigade? How could they be more than 100 per cent unserviceable?

The answer came from Lentaigne's Chief of Staff, Brigadier H. T. Alexander. The discrepancy was caused by less efficient investigation in 111. The situation in both Brigades was equally bad. Lentaigne added that the main trouble was the lack of officers, but he would do his best to fulfil General Stilwell's orders.

The orders were sent out as soon as the British party had left. Both Brigades were to continue with the tasks previously assigned, 'to the best of your ability', using 'all effectives. Ineffective, sick and wounded, will, as before, be evacuated.'

As Lentaigne did not believe there were many effectives, he took this order as giving him the priority he needed to evacuate the sick as he saw them, which was everyone in 111 and 77. Most of 111 set off for Kamaing and evacuation, and by 27 July, all of 111 Brigade would be on their way out. To Stilwell, this was insubordination all over again, effectually reinstating Lentaigne's own-initiative orders for replacing 111 Brigade with 14.

Vinegar Joe was furious, but powerless. As soon as Mountbatten heard about it, he sent Stilwell a radio message confirming the requirement to evacuate 77 and 111 Brigades, plus anybody else who was sick, and that 14 Brigade and the West Africans were to be taken out as soon as the British 36th Division were on the move, orders for which had already been issued.

Black Watch Battle Group Diary: *'July 16, 42 Col recce found that the ascent from Sahki was impassable for mules and spent the day cutting steps. Lt Hyde with the Burrifs pushed on to Pungan to find a harbour for the*

Cols. As they were leaving they contacted a Jap platoon which they engaged with Bren fire before withdrawing.'

Next day, two platoons of 42 Column set out at intervals up the track, in advance of the main party. One platoon walked unknowingly through a Jap ambush that was in the process of being deployed. The next platoon discovered the ambush and engaged the enemy until the leading group of 42 Column came up and joined in, all much hampered by a Jap machine gun trained on the track. The Jocks moved into the jungle to try and outflank the enemy and a grenade at least put the machine gun out of commission, but the jungle was too thick for further advancing. Fire from a three-inch mortar did the job and the Japs retreated, 'leaving a lot of blood and no wounded'.

The Pungan district was the objective, but several attempts failed to dislodge the enemy garrison in the village of Nugusharwng. Still the Jocks moved up in readiness for an attack, occupying a ridge above it, on top of a hill which, according to a Burrif guide, was just climbable:

'July 20, 73 Col Rifle Coy moved forward in the morning prepared for battle but despite the brief clashes the previous day, it was found that the enemy had moved out. Early in the afternoon it was reported that the village was clear and the remainder of both Cols followed on.'

For the next twelve days, the Jocks stayed in the Pungan area. Patrols were sent out, blocks were set up on the Pahok road, and routes were cleared and improved so that sick convoys could have an easier passage. There was an increase in supply drops, with fresh meat and vegetables to supplement the K rations and, in a seemingly irrelevant gesture, G. G. Green had Bill Lark's bagpipes sent over.

Physical deterioration in virtually all of the men, and the sickness, especially typhus, was such that the Battalion reached its lowest ever point of capability. The remaining medics did a count. The answer was that from the original 800, two officers and forty-eight other ranks could be classed as fit enough for work. Among them was Bill Lark:

'The little group of three of us, me, the mule sergeant and the mule vet, who was a sergeant as well and not really a vet but he understood about mules, used to make a special breakfast. I had a square tin from somewhere, and put our rations of biscuits in a bag and hammered them into crumbs, and a fruit bar or two crumbled up, and some water, and I used to cook it all up on a little stove which was a bully-beef tin filled with flame-thrower fuel. The result was like a pudding, something to fill you. So my two mates used to do a bit more of the mule stuff and I suppose I took on that role a little, of cook to the three of us, and I had a cooking place under the village hut (at Pungan) where we were assembling before Labu.

'Beside it I had a small pit where we kept our bully beef tins ready as stoves for the use of, covered with a bit of old sandbag, and I put my hand in to get a tin to make a brew. There was something in there which wasn't a tin. I pulled the sandbag back, and there was a socking great snake in there, lying all peaceful, so I got my bayonet and gave him such a whack, and he shot past me out into the open, and I shouted "Snake!" and the other lads finished him off. I suppose I must have slowed him down a bit.'

War Diary: '*July 25, the Yorks and Lancs passed through to a harbour a little further on. A party of REs went forward to bridge a chaung so that sick could be evacuated and the soft skins who were expected in a few days could join the Cols.*

177

> *'July 28, the first sick convoy passed through on the way to Pahok.'*

No man could have been but deeply moved by the sight of this convoy. Those just clinging to life were on ponies and mules, while those in slightly better condition were clinging to the animals or each other. As Jim McNeilly said, it reminded you of those pictures from the First World War, when lines of men who had been gassed and blinded staggered along with a hand on the next man's shoulder.

Bill Lark: 'A lot of the men had typhus, and one symptom is that you go deaf, so this Canadian doctor said he wanted the piper to come down and play at the sort of hospital they'd set up. Men were dying, but the idea was to instil the will to live in those who weren't dying yet.'

This moment is mentioned in the official medical report of the whole expedition:

'116 cases or 2.1 per cent of the total evacuation from sickness were admitted to hospital from this cause (typhus). Interrogation of medical officers after their return from Burma would indicate that a further 49 cases were diagnosed but were not flown out owing to recovery or death occurring before evacuation of the patient could be undertaken.

'The majority of the cases (77 per cent) belonged to 14 Brigade, in which sporadic outbreaks occurred from the beginning of May to the second week in August. In the other brigades, cases commenced to appear intermittently during the last 2 months of the campaign but mainly in July.

'The type of terrain in which these cases were infected varied considerably. The area in which infection must have occurred in the first outbreak, estimating the incubation period as 12 days, was mainly scrub jungle inter-spersed with open paddy-fields. The second minor epidemic broke out during the occupation of a village in which the troops were static for almost a month. However, the greater part of it was overrun with elephant grass and this location more closely resembled a jungle clearing than an inhabited locality. The third and most explosive outbreak could be traced to infection occurring during the occupation of a chaung (Black Watch and 7th Leicesters at Namkwin Chaung) in which the banks of the river were covered with thick elephant grass. In general from the evidence available, the type of terrain in which the majority of cases became infected was open country abounding in elephant grass and in the neighbourhood of water. No cases occurred in dense bamboo jungle, only in the scrub variety.

'The first cases to appear were generally diagnosed as glandular fever, being mild with little more than complaints of headache, feeling out of sorts, and some glandular enlargement. Several of these cases, especially during this early period and at a time when the possibility of typhus had not yet been fully appreciated, remained ambulatory throughout the whole of their attack, and recovered; this even occurred later when the disease had been fully recognised and diagnosed.

'It was not until the onset became more abrupt with a high temperature, which failed to respond to quinine, that typhus was fully suspected. Thereafter the severe constitutional upset, the red bloated face with intensely congested conjunctives; the prolonged fever without the intermittency of malaria, pyrexia, and the appearance of a macula-papular rash on the trunk 3 or 4 days later, left no doubt regarding the diagnosis in the minds of the medical officers.

'The progress of these cases caused generally grave anxiety. Pulmonary complications were generally severe, mental depression so profound that the patients appeared to have no desire to recover. This apathy was counteracted in the Black Watch to a very considerable extent when someone conceived the idea that the sound of the pipes might do much to dispel this apathy. Moreover, in the absence of specific treatment little could be done for these patients under the existing circumstances. Proper and efficient nursing was quite out of the question. Protection from the monsoon had to be improvised with indifferent success; fever became unbearable in the warm moist climate, and some patients lapsed into delirium; water was warm and brackish and great difficulty was experienced in forcing these patients to maintain their water and salt balance and avoid dehydration; diet was restricted to articles upon which the patients had existed for many months and which now produced intense nausea; the number of nursing orderlies was limited and they could not cope adequately with the number of cases.

'Under these circumstances, and in men already debilitated with prolonged marching and recurrent attacks of malaria, it is not surprising that mortality from this disease reached the high figures of 29.7 per cent . This high death rate was quickly appreciated by all ranks, and the subsequent fear of contracting the disease resulted in a substantial decrease in morale.'

Monsoon rains had delayed the soft skins' move out from their harbour until 21 July.
Diary states:

'July 22, probably the hardest day's march of the whole campaign. We covered two miles, climbing to 2,000 feet.

Bivouacked beside the 7th Leicesters whom we had caught up.'

There was no move the next day but they marched on the 24th, then stuck for two days. A makeshift hospital was put up where the sick would be left behind and news came that they were to join the battle groups at Ngusharawng, in the Pungan district, rather than Pahok.

On 25 July Stilwell called for another conference to clear up 'misunderstandings'. General Wedemeyer represented Mountbatten. Stilwell and Lentaigne made reluctant compromises. The very last remnants of 77 Brigade, some muleteers, were to be sent out immediately. The attack on Taungni would continue, and 14 Brigade would cover 111 while casualties were evacuated. Both 14 and 3rd West African Brigades were to stay in, fighting for Stilwell until after the fall of Myitkyina, but Lentaigne would keep Stilwell informed of their status.

After the usual time lag, the newspapers at home caught up with the action. This was the Scottish *Sunday Mail*:

'Lively Offensive Kept Up. Special Force troops (are) patrolling north of Taungni . . . adding to their recent outstanding work in wiping out strong pockets of resistance in the hills, N and NW of Taungni. Operating in the most difficult jungle country and in incessant monsoon downpour, they have been driving the enemy relentlessly south . . . men of the Black Watch and Yorks and Lancs regiments swept into the village of Nugusharwng, 7 miles NW of Taungni, on the morning of July 20. The Japanese fled taking their dead with them.

'An Associated Special Correspondent with the Allied Forces in N Burma says that the Chindits operating in

(the) Mogaung (Valley) in future will not be referred to as Chindits, but as the 3rd Indian Division or by regimental associations.'

On 27 July the Jocks' soft skins managed four miles in seven hours, to find 'huge ration and clothing dumps left by 111 Brigade'. Half an hour after they arrived at this point, Mawyang, there was a minor miracle. An aircraft dropped their mail. Letters from home. Alas, many of the addressees were no longer able to read their letters.

On 29 July after ten hours' marching, the Jocks were reunited.

War Diary: *'The soft skins – sadly depleted in numbers through sickness – rejoined the Col in the afternoon and evening. The REs also arrived back. July 31, sickness on the increase and typhus is taking its toll.'*

The assessment of the strength of 14, 111, and 3rd West African Brigades at this time showed that of 11,200 men – the total originally flown in with the replacements added as they went along – there remained 3,400. Total for the three brigades of killed, wounded, captured or missing was 1,300. Already evacuated or scheduled for it were almost 7,500. Those left and supposedly fit were in the lowest spirits, exhausted, and not much better in physical health than the ones checked in by the medics. Mental health could break down too.

Jim McNeilly: 'Yes, it happened, self-inflicted wounds, even the ultimate. Malaria combined with depression. The army didn't recognise depression, but those days and nights in the monsoon, and feeling useless, marching this way and that and getting nowhere, well, it got to some men. Can't blame them. How can you blame them? It was totally demoralising. I knew one laddie quite well, great big man, footballer, played for Scotland schoolboys, and I asked him, "What's wrong?" And he just said, "I'm ill," and turned away and walked off into the trees. Never saw him again.'

A day or so's march away from Pungan, Labu was an important village for control of the main Japanese northbound supply line, the Indaw railway. This was to be the Jocks' last objective. They would reinforce the equally depleted Yorks and Lancs who were already in the area, and they spent the first days of August resting before moving up on the 4th of the month.

War Diary: '*August 5, both Cols moved forward at 07.30 hrs intending to pass through the Y&L and push on to Labu. At about 09.30 hrs firing broke out on the right apparently from a small enemy force on a hill operation. Mortar fire was brought down on them and 42 Col Rifle Coy moved forward and linked up with the Y&L. There was sporadic firing all day.*

'*August 6, about mid-day 73 Col recce pl was ordered forward along the track to Labu. Some three hundred yards behind the Y&L perimeter they hit a strongly dug-in Jap platoon. After calling up the 42 Col Rifle Coy, the recce platoon withdrew after suffering four casualties.*'

All that was left of the 42 rifle company were three very weak platoons and just one platoon officer, Lieutenant Wynne. On that afternoon of 6 August, their assault progressed a little but they had to give up. Douglas Donald Wynne, on attachment from the Seaforth Highlanders, was killed attacking a machine gun. At nightfall, 73 Column rifle company relieved them.

Next morning, they and any other remnants of 73 Column tried to flush the enemy out. There were three officers – Major Ross, Lieutenant R. J. Noble – who had been until now animal transport officer with the soft skins and a strong leader in their long march – and Lt. A. Gibb, previously RSM, commissioned in the field two weeks before.

A scouting party found the Japs had retreated a little from their positions of the day before, and so an early attempt was made to capitalise. It was 06.45, 7 August 1944, almost six months since they landed at Aberdeen airstrip.

Jim McNeilly: 'The Japs were very well set and they blasted us straightaway. A machine gun opened up and I was hit in the leg which smashed the bone, and we had quite a few more wounded although not in my section, but the Sergeant said keep going, get that machine gun. One man lost both his legs, and we had to be taken back to the hut where the medics were. They rearranged my leg how it should be and tied my two legs together with string. I had to have it redone when we got back to India.'

The Japanese often issued reports and general instructions to their troops, which had to be learned by heart. Here is one such, and very appropriate it is:

'The hostile forces are skilled in approaching by crawling, and they often get within 15 yards of our troops without being detected. They open surprise fire with very rapid-firing automatic weapons and deal destructive blows. However, they do not charge; their grenade throwers approach and toss grenades or shoot them with grenade rifles. If our positions are held strongly, the opposing forces will retreat after a short time, or they may send combat details around our flanks to attack with grenades and automatic weapons.'

Mortars and more pressure forced the enemy off the ridge and into a back line of deep trenches from which they could not be shifted, and by late afternoon it was stalemate. Colonel

Green ordered one last push and called up Pipe Corporal Lark.

Jim McNeilly: 'We used to kid him on, Piper Lark, calling him the minister and Brother Lark. He was devout, and had been since Palestine. Never fired a shot, as far as I know, but he was some man for all that.'

Bill Lark: 'I was on the path, had to be. I couldn't play the pipes in the jungle, I'd have got in a tangle. There were men on either side, our men, in among the trees. Maybe the Japs could see me, I don't know, I never saw them. I just played, but I can't remember what I played, probably "The Black Bear."'

If anyone ever has doubts about the effect that the skirl of the pipes can have on Scottish soldiers, even in the direst circumstances, the story of the next few minutes will surely dispel them.

Bill Lark: 'One of our lads said to me afterwards about Corporal Walter Graham, that we called Watty, who heard the pipes and said to his section, "Come on boys, we're going in." They'd all been miserable up to that point, pinned down, not knowing what was going to happen. One of them said, "What about the Japs?" So Watty said, "Fuck the Japs, we're going in."'

They did go in, led by Lieutenant Noble. Not all of them still had a bayonet to fix, but they went anyway.

Bill Lark: 'One fellow said afterwards, it was the pipes that did it. Another said aye, the Japs could na stand it.'

The last word on the battle for Nabu should go to a member of the Yorks and Lancs, name unknown, who saw the whole thing:

'We were still held up and it was decided to call up some of the Black Watch column which was behind us to help out. Imagine our amazement when we heard the sound of the bagpipes, followed in a few minutes by bayonets-fixed Jocks

185

who went down the track towards the Jap positions with the piper giving forth with all his might. The lads charged, screaming and so on, and the Japs took off. I strongly suspect it was the pipes that frightened them, not the bayonets. That piper, unarmed except for his pipes, was as near a hero as anyone I ever knew.'

War Diary: '*August 7, 73 Col joined battle early in the morning and by the evening with spirits high and pipes playing had cleared the enemy from the village.*'

The Scottish *Daily Record*, almost two months later, saw the episode in a more dramatic light:

'Bayonet Charge On Japs With "Hampden Roar".
With bagpipes skirling madly, and with a roar reminiscent of Hampden on International Day, the Black Watch routed a Jap force in the recent Burma fighting with one of the fiercest bayonet charges in history.

'*This taste of cold steel in the Highland fashion completely demoralised the yellow men and, as the Black Watch padre from Aberdeen said afterwards: "It was undoubtedly the most thrilling action of their whole North Burma campaign."*

'*This was the blow that drove the enemy out of the hills flanking the west side of the Mogaung-Mandalay road and railway, to secure those strategic heights while the all-British 36th Division advanced on Taungni and Pinbaw, south of Mogaung.*

'*. . . within a few hundred yards of the village, enfilade fire made further progress impossible. So Lieut. Jack Noble, of Dalkeith, was ordered to take his platoon on a flanking move to the left, with the object of clearing*

186

strong machine-gun nests . . . all was set for a final attack.

'A last dramatic touch was the calling for the pipes, which struck up the regimental march, "Hielan' Laddie".

"'I gave the order to fix bayonets," said Lieut. Noble, "and with all the automatic weapons up in the front, we went in at the double. We gave them everything we had, and the Japs got up and bolted rather than face our bayonets."

'Shortly afterwards, the men who had gone in with the bayonet joined other members of the company in a simple but impressive funeral service, conducted by the Padre, Captain the Rev. S. B. Mair.

'As the padre read out the names, Pipe Corporal Wm. Lark played "The Flowers of the Forest".'

The Battalion stayed in Labu for ten days. The sick and wounded were evacuated and the Battalion was reformed out of its columns and into more orthodox dispositions. They managed to make two rather sparse companies:

'August 16, B Coy under Major Frazer paraded for drill in the morning but after about ten minutes a supply drop on the parade ground, the only open space in the jungle, caused the parade to break up. On the following morning the time of the parade was changed and so, fortunately some thought, was the supply drop.

'August 17, Battalion moved from Labu in the early morning, into the staging camp at Pahok. On the way we passed through 36 Division moving forward and were thankful that our part was about over. The heat was intense, about 119 degrees, and the hard road was something to which we were not used.'

Bill Lark: 'I stood with the colonel as the men came along a main road, playing the march-past for each company, what there was of them, and my own C-Company tune, "Lawson's Men".'

War Diary: *'August 18, Battalion left for Mogaung at 02.30 hrs to avoid marching in the heat of the day, and arrived there at 07.30 hrs. After breakfast, A Coy and Bn HQ moved by jeep train (jeeps adapted to run on railway lines) to Myitkyina and arrived at 11.00 hrs.'*

They didn't entirely avoid the noonday sun.

Bill Lark: 'After all that, we had to walk from the station to the airstrip. Talk about hot. We were shattered, really. Somebody said "Can't we wait for the next bus?" but G. G. Green was there, and he told me to get to the front and play my pipes again. We reached the airstrip without anyone dropping down, and there were the Dakotas. Heavenly chariots. We could hardly believe it. No Japs, no leeches, no K rations, no mud up to our knees. G. G. Green was first aboard.'

War Diary: *'The first plane took off at 14.15 hrs and the CO reached Dinjan where the rest of the Coy came in at intervals. They were taken to Tinsukia reception camp (US army establishment outside this city in tea-growing area of Assam).'*

Meanwhile, B Company was moving by jeep train from Mogaung to Myitkyina, but they had transport from the station to the airstrip.

'August 19, by mid-day everyone was in the reception camp where hot showers and new clothing made a great difference.'

Another long journey awaited the Jocks, to Bangalore, which took twelve days, and here was a great sorting out, with repatriations, reorganisations, leave, and a look to the future as an airborne battalion under Major Ross. At the end of September there was to be a party at the Viceroy's palace in Simla, one of the great hill stations of the Raj and the Viceroy's summer capital.

Bill Lark: 'It was called "The Lodge", but it looked more like one of those big Victorian hotels at the seaside. There was a Chinese delegation there, featuring Generalissimo Chiang Kai-Shek, and I had to play the pipes and say the health in Gaelic, thereupon downing a glass of whisky. I didn't drink, I'd never had whisky. I had no idea what would happen to me if I did have it, so I asked the butler. He fixed me up with a glass of cold tea and I quaffed that.'

Chapter Nine

Post Mortem

The Jocks and most of the other Chindits withdrawing at this time were concentrated in the reception camp at Tinsukia. Besides the obvious luxuries of hot baths and new, dry, clothes, they were gently introduced to proper feeding again by a special convalescent type of rations which, according to those being subjected to the regime, seemed to feature rather a lot of chicken soup.

Not featuring so in the campaign was a psychiatrist, now on attachment to Special Force, who interviewed as many of the men as he could to try to gauge the effect the campaign had had mentally, and to learn what might be useful for any similar expeditions in the future.

His reports on the different brigades show one thing clearly, and that was concerning over-all morale. Those units which had finished their operations with a success, a win in a fight with the Japs, such as the Black Watch, were in better spirits than those who had not, or who had suffered some sort of reverse at the last.

Such a finding will not surprise many ordinary observers of human activity, but that's psychiatry for you.

The doctor was himself surprised by the general good level of morale, considering how long the men had been in the jungle and the suffering they had been through. Perhaps he did not attach sufficient importance to the parallel phenomenon of banging one's head against a brick wall. It's great when you stop.

During August and September, he examined 372 men of 14 Brigade, being 126 2nd Battalion Black Watch, 88 of the 7th Leicesters, 84 of the 1st Beds and Herts, and 74 of the 2nd Yorks and Lancs. This is part of his report:

'Psychiatric Casualties: No case of psychiatric illness was seen on personal contact or referred by Camp. M.O., Bn. M.O.s or local hospitals.

'Factors influencing Morale Unfavourably:

(a) Promises. Black Watch and Y & L personnel complained bitterly of official promises of their 'going out', which never materialised. Every job after May was their last job and morale dropped considerably with each promise. In marked contrast the other two bns stated they never had one official promise throughout the campaign and suffered no loss of morale in consequence.

(b) Reinforcements. All stated they were never up to full strength and an increased burden was thus thrown on remaining personnel of unit. Many of the reinforcements received were untrained in jungle warfare and had never seen a heavy pack.

(c) Length of Campaign. Much too long. If the campaign had terminated before the monsoon many deaths from illness would have been avoided and all felt they would have been in a better mood to face a second campaign than they are now.

(d) Rations. K rations monotonous and almost unbearable after three months.

(e) Officers. "Class-distinction" too much in

191

evidence, particularly regarding monsoon equipment and medical evacuation.'

The Black Watch men might well have mentioned those
American hammocks, and officers on horseback, including
Colonel Green, and an incident in which a man was
upbraided for carrying a junior officer's pack. The Jocks
around this officer, including Jim McNeilly, were taking it in
turns to help him out, as he was so weak.

Jim McNeilly: 'I think he must have had malaria at the time,
which we all got. It wasn't like some did and some didn't. We
all did, and more than once. Anyway, G. G. Green says
"What are you carrying his pack for?" and the boy turns
round and salutes, mind you, salutes, and says "I'll carry his
fucking pack if I want to." So the colonel had all the officers
and NCOs in for a meeting about discipline, especially the
captain, who'd said to him "It's all right for you, sitting up
there on your arse." '

Report continues:

(f) **Medical Inspections. Not one individual but
complained of having had no proper medical
"over-haul" before he went in. Some had none at
all. Others were actually checked for fitness by a
Sgt-Major consulting pay-books. They have had
no medical inspection since leaving Burma. The
general feeling, resultant on this, is that they are
of the opinion that no one cares how they feel and
that they have been neglected.**

(g) **Medical Treatment. Despite the admirable efforts
of the M.O.s (with two exceptions) treatment was
described variously as inadequate to ridiculous to
call it treatment at all. It was common for sick to
be turned away by the M.O. with the apology**

192

that he had nothing to give them. On occasion it was impossible to get even a bandage, parachute cloth having ultimately to be torn up to serve the purpose. Coln. 16 of Bedfs Herts complained of having no M.O. at all for 6 weeks. A L/Cpl. (from the Bn) carried on in his absence and it was rather alarming to learn from the Cpl himself that he was giving intravenous quinines, pentathols and performing minor operations on his own.

(h) Unknown Fever (Scrub Typhus). Without exception this affected the morale of the men considerably. They saw friends "dying like flies" with the fever and in cases they were even afraid to visit those stricken with the fever for fear of contracting it themselves.

(i) Medical Evacuation. None had any great confidence of getting evacuated if sick. Indeed the one concern in the mind of each individual was the fear of falling sick with the disturbing prospect of having to endure hardships in the coln were he unfit.

(j) Age and Weight. A considerable bond of sympathy existed between the men and those they considered overage and underweight. Men of 38 and 39 they believe should never have been sent in, and it was ridiculous to have included men of little more than 8 stone in weight. Giving the weight of the heavy pack as 69 to 81lbs this meant those men were carrying over half to three quarters of their own weight. They blame this on the lackadaisical medical inspection prior to entering the campaign.

(k) Defective Vision. Those wearing glasses definitely did not possess the confidence of the men whose visual acuity was good. They went in constant fear of either losing or breaking their glasses, and even with them on the glasses were often little better than useless owing to rain and perspiration dimming the lenses. (An M.O. from personal experience gave it as his opinion that this latter observation was a very real one.)

Factors Favourably Influencing Morale.

(1)   Self-appreciation. All bns could point with some pride to the part they had played in the campaign. They feel they have achieved what they set out to accomplish and are solid in their assertions that the Jap is anything but invincible and "has it coming to him".

Addendum. Prior to the campaign a considerable number of men were put up by S.M.O. and Bn. M.O.s for regrading (as unsuitable), but many of these were turned down by Medical Boards. S.M.O. maintains that Specialists in hospitals are not fully conversant with the true conditions obtaining in the field and that less stress should be put on their findings and more on those of Bn. M.O.s. Those originally put up for regrading by him and his staff were ultimately evacuated as unfit during the campaign.'

The psychiatrist concluded that morale in general was good, and that the unanimous opinion of the men was that they thought they would be all right for another go in six months. We may speculate as to whether an army psychiatrist at that time had the same attitude to mental pain as the legendary army dentists had to the physical kind, and what the patients of either might have expected in the way of tea and sympathy.

So, the men thought they had done well, achieving what

was asked of them, and perhaps they were even ready to do it again – but what was the reality, looking out of the big window of the strategists and high commanders, rather than looking up from the floor of the jungle?

We know that a lot of reverse civil engineering was done – bridges blown, roads and railways broken – but we don't know how seriously this inconvenienced the enemy. We know that numbers of Japanese soldiers and officers were killed and wounded, but we don't know how many. Certainly the figure would not compare with losses in a major pitched battle, for example the one at Imphal and Kohima, going on at much the same time, where foolish and risk-taking leadership gave the Japanese 55,000 casualties, including 13,500 dead, many of which, like Chindit losses, were from the combined forces of disease, exhaustion and malnutrition.

The Japanese were quite willing to admit, after the war, that the two Chindit expeditions had been taken seriously and had been far more than just an irritant. Suddenly finding British troops operating as they pleased, on the 'wrong' side of the Chindwin River, had caused great consternation among Jap generals. Only days before General Mutaguchi planned to launch his attack on Assam, the first airborne Chindits went in. Some in the Jap high command were for turning their attention to this new threat, dealing with it and returning later to the invasion of India. Mutaguchi pointed out that when he had taken Assam, he would have all the airfields currently supplying these impudent jungle British, so there was no point in worrying about them. Even so, some troops in the Japanese strategic reserve were brought up to attack White City and the other strongholds, men who otherwise would have been deployed elsewhere.

The most important general contribution by the Chindits, in the view of the Japanese, was to make Japan's defence of her conquests in north Burma much more difficult. Her soldiers were sandwiched between Stilwell and Special Force. They could not advance against the US/Chinese army, neither could they hold the Mogaung-Myitkyina line as they intended to do. With their supply lines constantly being cut and their troops south of Mogaung occupied with the marauding Chindits, the Japs were forced to fall back, leaving Myitkyina free for the 36th Division to land and march south to meet them and, eventually, to drive them out of Burma.

American and some British evaluations of the Chindit effect don't even go that far. Stilwell never thought they did anything very much at all, either with Jap communications, or by inflicting casualties in numbers that mattered. Slim said much the same, believing that the columns were too lightly armed to do serious damage and the strongholds similarly ill-equipped to take on the enemy in significant battles. For Stilwell, Special Force seemed always too far away to render direct service to him and his Chinese, and later on it was too sick to do anything anyway.

As if that were not enough evidence of failure, they had the statistics. The Chindits seemed to have paid a very heavy price for their achievements. Here are the numbers for 14 Brigade:

	Officers	*Other ranks*
Fly-in strength	176	3,295
Replacements	9	153
Total strength	185	3,348
Killed	12	99
Wounded	14	162
Sick (hospitalised)	39	381
Captured	0	0
Missing	2	27
Sick/wounded for evac.	29	1,098
Total loss	96	1,967
Total effectives flown out	89	1,481

196

For 111 Brigade, the figures are even worse:

	Officers	Other ranks
Fly-in strength	163	3,553
Replacements	30	398
Total strength	193	3,951
Killed	15	186
Wounded	34	373
Sick (hospitalised)	49	1,182
Captured	1	10
Missing	8	171
Sick/wounded for evac.	78	1,853
Total loss	*175*	*3,375*
Total effectives flown out	*8*	*176*

The summary figures in Mountbatten's final report for the whole of Operation Thursday were 1,035 killed; 2,531 wounded; 473 missing; 7,217 hospital admissions, that is forty per cent of Special Force, three-quarters of which were due to disease. Of those 'effectives' examined, fifty per cent were declared unfit for active service.

These figures do not include those who fell sick in the column and who might normally have been hospitalised or evacuated, but who could not be for various reasons. Some of them died, some recovered to a greater or less extent and marched on. Such cases were treated by the medical officer, for example of malaria, dysentery and minor 'civilian' maladies such as tonsillitis and tooth abscesses, of which field medical units normally see large numbers. There are no statistics for these cases because the column MOs largely didn't report them.

It was recommended by the senior medics that in future men should be evacuated in their third attack of malaria so that they could be properly treated in hospital and flown back in when they recovered.

Stilwell's writings, and notes of his conversations, show a total disregard for the Chindits, both officers and men. He thought they were idiots, and useless idiots at that. He accused the senior officers of disobeying orders and threatened them with official complaints to higher authority. He had said to Lentaigne: 'I intend to make a case out of this. You are not obeying orders.'

The British press, Stilwell noted, took every opportunity to hail the Chindit hero without ever mentioning the achievements of his Chinese and Americans – which, he was sure, would soon eclipse anything the Brits had done. When he did give credit to the Chindits, it was grudgingly, and in terms meaning that they had only managed to carry out orders and, for a change, hadn't made a mess of it.

'If only Wingate had lived' has been the conventional response to Chindit criticism from earliest days. He died before Special Force was properly established, and his successor, Lentaigne, despite having been through the training and commanding a Chindit brigade, was not a believer. He thought Wingate a maverick, a renegade, and in any case was not privy to much of his former leader's operational intentions, which were complex to say the least. Without Wingate's influence, stature and zeal as Chindit Prophet, Lentaigne could not make it work. It was too difficult. He was the test pilot who didn't trust his new aircraft.

In any case, maybe the job was too difficult, full stop. Maybe even Wingate would have found it so, far away from his hugely complicated network of measures and countermeasures, trying to solve a fantastical, constantly moving crossword puzzle with incomplete clues that came by wireless and no real idea where the blank squares were. As early as 15 May, *The Times* had been expressing doubts about Stilwell's strategy:

'Monsoon Limitations. Indian opinion does not know quite what to make of the military operations in Burma and Assam which, although the monsoon is almost on us, are still to all appearances in a highly inconclusive state. While it is accepted that the Japanese offensive has shot its bolt for this campaigning season, there is a good deal of speculation on the extent to which the allies are likely to gain the objectives they have set themselves.

'Those objectives, admittedly, have not been more closely defined than as the clearance of as much of northern Burma as is necessary to enable the construction of the Ledo road to proceed. This is taken to imply an intention on General Stilwell's part to get as far south as Mogaung and Myitkyina . . . towns in which General Stilwell could sit in relative comfort during the monsoon and, it is believed, in fair security in view of the cutting of communications between northern and southern Burma, and of the destruction of Japanese ammunition, food and oil dumps in central Burma by Major-General Lentaigne's penetration troops.'

However, *The Times* correspondent pointed out, Stilwell had not been able to advance on Mogaung. The Japanese were not giving an inch:

'In the Japanese rear, fighting was reported in a recent SEAC statement to have taken place at a point south of Mogaung. It is deduced from this that part of General Lentaigne's Special Force, which had not previously been heard of anywhere near Mogaung, has moved north to give General Stilwell closer support. (This development) may accelerate General Stilwell's advance but, on the other hand, the weather must by now be slowing all troop movements.'

199

Too little, too late is the expression that comes to mind. Too late was concluded with the long march by 16 Brigade, so that exhausted troops could do little to shift the Japs at Indaw and, when they did shift them, it didn't seem to matter. Too late was 14 Brigade going in because there were no Dakotas available, all being deployed elsewhere, so the Jocks and the rest couldn't get to 77 and 111 Brigades when they needed help in May.

This is all true, but the greatest enemy of the Chindits was the one given the least attention at the time and, largely, since – sickness. The entire expedition was a medical catastrophe. It is incontestable that Special Force was more effective before the monsoon than after, when it could perform much better as a collection of hit-and-run units. Later, large parts of the force were more stationary, in bad country, in the monsoon – and sickness destroyed them. Was that unavoidable? For the time, was the medical service up to the mark? Did the men themselves understand what the tropics could do?

During the campaign, a third of the total Chindit strength was admitted to hospital for sickness, three times the number of those admitted for wounds, and many of the wounded were sick too. Of the remainder, more than half were hospitalised after they came out of Burma.

These are averages. The sick:wounded ratio was most pronounced in 14 Brigade. The cause is simple to find. The role given to the Black Watch and their comrade battalions was one of continuous, utterly exhausting marches hither and thither, knee deep in water and mud, which contributed hugely to infection by typhus, which the other brigades hardly suffered from.

Scrub typhus appeared in 14 Brigade near the beginning of May. At first, there were just a few cases of this disease with no name, but over the month there were more and more, and by the end of May there had been over fifty cases, some of them fatal. Individual cases kept on occurring until mid-August, when there was a sizeable outbreak confined mainly to the Black Watch Battalion. The death rate, as we have seen, was almost 30 per cent.

In all cases, leading to death or recovery, there was a long period of fever during which the sick man could do almost nothing. Not surprisingly, the mystery disease acquired an extra dimension. Those contracting it knew what was going to happen.

On top of the typhus, the major ailments leading eventually to evacuation were of course malaria, and towards the end, jungle sores, and the increase in all sickness can be associated with the type of activity the men were asked to perform. For example, the rate of sickness losses among the Jocks in April and May, while they were patrolling, fighting and moving almost daily, was increasing but steadily. It was bearable, the sickness, even if the replacements for evacuees were not entirely to everyone's liking. However, when the Second Battalion was given more duties patrolling from a stable base, the rate of sickness shot up. Compare the figures:

14 Brigade, 20 March to 3 June:
 Killed 71, wounded 95, missing 27, sick evacuated 151, total 344.

14 Brigade final figures:
 Killed 111, wounded 176, missing 29, sick evacuated or waiting for same, 1,547.

From the medical point of view, there were more influences at work than the physical ones. Getting better from sickness is partly to do with the will to get better. Doctors pointed to the morale of a force conceived as "Special", one which could strike and disappear, ready to strike again where least expected. So long as this was what they were doing and being, morale – and the will to get better – remained strong. Once downgraded, as it were, to be more conventional colleagues of Chinese and Americans, there was a certain sense of depreciation.

Before that, there can be no question that the monsoon rains were a more stringent test of general morale and medical discipline than anyone foresaw. Mosquitos and mites, water contamination, poor sanitation, jungle sores, just about everything bad, doubled and tripled in the rain. The consequences of the work and the rations, weight loss, vitamin deficiency and loss of appetite all lead to a downward spiral of fatigue and carelessness with personal sanitation, and mostly happened towards the end.

If we take the incidence of malaria, the story is clear. Perfect discipline with the malaria tablets could not have prevented malaria symptoms entirely, but would it have kept them down to 'acceptable' levels? The rate rose all the way through the campaign but doubled in July compared with May and June. By August, malaria cases were running between six and nine times higher than in April, and that is only from the numbers reported by the column MOs. The estimate from later analysis is that there were almost as many unreported cases. One conclusion is that Special Force gave up on the Atabrine. As an example, there was an incident outside the Second Battalion where three men died of cerebral malaria, and their packs were found to contain all their current supplies of tablets. Another conclusion is that Atabrine was not good enough for men so weakened.

In the circumstances, the Jocks and the other Chindits achieved near miracles of endurance and military success. We have to wonder what more they might have achieved if they had taken more care with their own well-being or, indeed, if they could have taken more care.

In any future campaigns of this sort, taking the evidence from the Chindit experiment, where it seemed everyone was taking part unknowingly in a clinical trial as well as fighting the Japs, it was concluded that there had to be a proper medical organisation capable of dealing with the human consequences. Medical personnel would have to be specially trained technically, and be able to cope physically with the business of the LRPGs. Officers and men would have to be made to realise that disease was a worse enemy than the Japanese and that every possible measure had to be taken to prevent it.

Rations sufficient for the work were essential, obviously, and interesting enough as food for the men to want to consume them and keep on consuming them. Good food means higher morale. This, of all the lessons of the experiment, was the easiest to learn and implement.

Perfect discipline with Mepacrine/Atabrine tablets is only possible if the supply is perfect. If the supply is irregular, no amount of discipline in the column can be enough.

Senior medical officers must be included when plans are made, and must be listened to, rather than being regarded as something of a nuisance as is traditional. Similarly, in the field, commanders must confide in, and respect the views of, medical officers.

Colonel Officer: 'One definite lesson learnt from this campaign is that three months is the very maximum period during which personnel can undertake this type of operation, and even this period must be reduced if carried out under monsoon conditions.'

That was all said after the event. Partly because of Wingate's attitude, and Stilwell's, and partly because the Chindits were going into unknown territory in all senses, the officers and men of the Second Battalion Black Watch and the 1st Cameronians, and every other soldier who went

203

into Burma in the Spring of 1944, were more than just pioneers of jungle warfare. They were unwitting volunteers in a gigantic, disorganised, unintentional medical experiment.

'Welfare of Troops in Burma. Lord Munster's Visit. Bombay, Oct. 24. Lord Munster, Parliamentary Under-Secretary of State for India, landed at an airstrip hacked out of the Burma jungle to discuss questions relating to the welfare of troops . . . During a three-hour meeting they dealt with many problems that have arisen in the past and situations which are likely to arise as our troops drive deeper into Burma. Leave, canteens, entertainment, repatriation and post-war prospects, difficulties of travel, provision of wireless sets and gramophones, and the effect on family life of long separations, all figured in the conversations. The work of such organisations as Toc H, the YMCA and the WVS was commended.'

The Times, October 1944

Sources

Interviews and conversations with David Rose, James McNeilly and William Lark.

Documents held at Black Watch Regimental HQ, Perth, and by the Ministry of Defence.

US Army Medical Department, Office of Medical History (including extracts from the Stilwell Papers).

Various newspapers, including *The Times, Sunday Mail, Daily Record.*

Imperial War Museum.

Barclay, Brigadier C.N. *The History of the Cameronians.*

Chinnery, Philip D. *March or Die.*

Cochran, Stewart. *Chindit.*

Fergusson, Bernard. *The Black Watch and the King's Enemies.*

Patterson, Frederick C. *From Rattray and Beyond.*

Rolo, Charles J. *Wingate's Raiders.*

Sykes, Christopher. *Orde Wingate.*

Various authors. *The Covenanter (*magazine of the Cameronians*).*

Index